Phase Transition in Korea-U.S. Science and Technology Relations

Caroline Wagner, Anny Wong, SungHo Lee,
Irene Brahmakulam

Prepared for Government of the Republic of Korea

RAND Science and Technology

The research described in this report was conducted by RAND Science and Technology for the Government of the Republic of Korea.

Library of Congress Cataloging-in-Publication Data

Phase transition in Korea–U.S. science and technology relations / Caroline Wagner ... [et al.].
     p. cm.
     "MR-1644."
     Includes bibliographical references.
     ISBN 0-8330-3333-6 (pbk.)
     1. Research—United States—International cooperation. 2. Research—Korea—
International cooperation. 3. Technology—United States—International cooperation. 4.
Technology—Korea—International cooperation. I. Wagner, Caroline S. II. Rand
Corporation.

Q180.U5P48 2003
338.973'06—dc21

                                                                        2002155705

RAND is a nonprofit institution that helps improve policy and decisionmaking through research and analysis. RAND® is a registered trademark. RAND's publications do not necessarily reflect the opinions or policies of its research sponsors.

Published 2003 by RAND
1700 Main Street, P.O. Box 2138, Santa Monica, CA 90407-2138
1200 South Hayes Street, Arlington, VA 22202-5050
201 North Craig Street, Suite 202, Pittsburgh, PA 15213-1516
RAND URL: http://www.rand.org/
To order RAND documents or to obtain additional information, contact Distribution
Services: Telephone: (310) 451-7002; Fax: (310) 451-6915; Email: order@rand.org

Preface

This report presents an analysis of the relationship between the Republic of Korea and the United States in science and technology (S&T). The research was conducted within the Science and Technology Division of RAND. The Korean Science and Engineering Foundation (KOSEF) requested the study, and the research was conducted in close cooperation with the Science and Technology Policy Institute of Korea (STEPI). The goal of this study is to provide input to the science policy decisions of both the United States and Korean governments.

RAND Science and Technology is a division focusing on research and analysis to improve government policy decisions. Comments on this report may be transmitted to Dr. Stephen Rattien, Director, RAND Science and Technology. Comments may also be transmitted to Dr. Sungchul Chung, at the Science and Technology Policy Institute, Seoul, Korea.

RAND Science and Technology
1200 South Hayes Street
Arlington, Virginia 22202-5050
703-413-1100

Contents

Figures

Tables

Summary

The governments of the Republic of Korea and the United States have made commitments to build a cooperative relationship in S&T that serves both political and scientific goals. The policy commitment, implemented over a 20-year period, has resulted in a strong S&T relationship. Partly as a result of this commitment, and partly due to Korea's aggressive investments into research and development (R&D) spending, Korean capacity to conduct world-class R&D now puts it among the top countries in the world. The record of its scientists publishing papers in international journals, as well as the registration of Korean patents, suggests that Korea has emerged from a pack of developing nations into the group of "scientifically advanced countries."

Both governments have made significant financial commitments to S&T cooperation. The Korean government's part in this effort has included investments in joint projects with the United States, supported by a policy of strong domestic investment in R&D. The United States government has provided both development assistance (now terminated) and special grant programs to build scientific capacity in Korea and to encourage cooperation. Thousands of Korean students have studied S&T in the United States. The result has been that, despite its relatively small size, Korea is among the U.S. government's top 20 partners in international cooperation in research and development (ICRD), and the United States is Korea's foremost ICRD partner.

The bilateral S&T relationship has grown in an environment where international S&T cooperation is growing overall: Promoting cooperation is becoming a more important part of the S&T policies of most advanced and many developing countries. The network resulting from international cooperation in science is creating a system that is transcending the actions and direct influence of individual nations, and taking on a global character. Both Korea and the United States are active partners with other countries in global science, and the bilateral relationship is being affected by the internationalization of S&T.

The enhanced scientific capacity of Korea, the changing structure of international science, and shifts in the role of the United States in it, suggest that a reexamination of the relationship is in order. Our research leads us to conclude that, while it may be fruitful to seed bilateral cooperation within policy programs, in fact, the most robust cooperation grows "from the bottom up"—

scientists linking with each other and identifying important areas of common interest and concern. Moreover, while it may be useful to continue to seek *bilateral* ties, international cooperation is more often taking on a *multinational* character. This suggests that a focus on a bilateral relationship may be too narrow: The two countries should look together at ways to link (jointly or separately) with other partners.

Opportunities for enhancing the relationship at the policy level exist but should be prioritized: International cooperation takes many forms and governments have only a limited ability to direct the flow and direction of scientific research. Governments have the most influence over large-scale "megascience" projects, such as an international high-energy physics lab. However, these projects tend to be expensive and of long duration. They require a great deal of "lobbying" to encourage investments in cooperation. Korea and the United States may wish to evaluate existing megascience activities, and discuss whether they should jointly consider (and propose) other such projects in the future.

Government policymakers also have influence over the creation and direction of distributed, organized research projects, such as the Intelligent Manufacturing Systems Project. Korea and the United States may wish to evaluate how well their joint participation in projects like these has worked, and discuss whether there are other subjects worth considering for this type of cooperative effort. These projects have the advantage over megascience projects of taking place in existing national labs and using information and communications technologies to enable collaboration. This means that less up-front investment is needed. The effort to maintain communication in a distributed collaboration, however, is more challenging than for a centrally located megascience project.

Governments have least influence over the links established by individual scientists seeking to enhance their own research activities. These projects tend to develop spontaneously from the interests of scientists themselves. Our research shows that many of these projects begin because scientists met each other face-to-face at conferences and international symposia. This would suggest that the sponsorship of joint meetings around specific subjects is a positive use of government resources when the goal is to encourage linkages at the level of the practitioner.

Both countries have "centers of excellence" that include geographically tied capabilities (such as information technology research in North Carolina) as well as intellectually driven capacities (such as Korean excellence in chemistry). Moreover, each country has made investments in scientific infrastructure that may be complementary with the capacities of the other. Mapping out these real and virtual "centers of excellence" and comparing them to existing activities is one way to identify target areas where cooperation may be fruitful in the future. Comparing national policies in R&D funding allocation and sharing ideas about emerging areas of importance in S&T are activities that would benefit both countries.

Forging a more balanced relationship in the future will require a move toward equal participation in initiation, management, and funding of joint activities. These activities should grow out of strengths, specializations, and joint concerns, rather than an interest in building capacity. A dialogue on scientific infrastructure with a focus on sharing and leveraging expensive resources would be one way to achieve balance. Using information and communications technologies more effectively to encourage sharing of knowledge and research capacity is another way to level the playing field. A continued dialogue about effective science policy, to include governance of controversial new technologies, could serve as a leadership model for other countries. A joint effort to identify scientific goals, and then to include other scientifically advanced countries in joint projects, would help to expand the relationship in ways that benefit the S&T base of both countries.

Abbreviations

AID	Agency for International Development (U.S.)
APCTP	Asia Pacific Center for Theoretical Physics
APEC	Asia Pacific Economic Cooperation
ASEAN	Association of Southeast Asian Nations
ASTN	APEC Science and Technology Network
CDC	Centers for Disease Control and Prevention (U.S.)
CERN	Center for European Nuclear Research
CIS	Commonwealth of Independent States
DoC	Department of Commerce (U.S.)
DoD	Department of Defense (U.S.)
DoE	Department of Energy (U.S.)
DoI	Department of the Interior (U.S.)
DoS	Department of State (U.S.)
DVA	Department of Veterans Affairs (U.S.)
ECOTECH	APEC Economic and Technology Cooperation
EDI	Electronic Data Interchange
EPA	Environmental Protection Agency (U.S.)
ERC	Engineering Research Center
GERD	Gross Expenditures on Research and Development
GRI	Government Research Institute
GSN	Global Seismograph Network
HAN Project	Highly Advanced National Project
HHS	Department of Health and Human Services (U.S.)
HPP	High Power Processing
IBGP	International Geosphere-Biosphere Program
ICRD	International Collaboration in Research and Development
ICT	Information and Communication Technologies
IMD	International Institute of Management Development
IMF	International Monetary Fund
IMS	Intelligent Manufacturing Systems

IPR	Intellectual Property Right
ISDN	Integrated Services Digital Network
ISS	International Space Station
ISTA	International Science and Technology Agreement
ITEP	Institute for Industrial Technology Evaluation and Planning (Korea)
ITER	International Thermonuclear Experimental Reactor
KIAS	Korea Institute for Advanced Studies
KIMM	Korea Institute of Machinery and Materials
KISTEP	Korea Institute of Science and Technology Evaluation and Planning
KOSEF	Korean Science and Engineering Foundation
KOSEN	Korean Science and Engineering Network (Korea)
KSEA	Korean-American Scientists and Engineers Association
LHC	Large Hadron Collider
MIT	Massachusetts Institute of Technology
MOCIE	Ministry of Commerce, Industry and Energy (Korea)
MOST	Ministry of Science and Technology (Korea)
MOU	Memorandum of Understanding
NASA	National Aeronautics and Space Administration (U.S.)
NIE	Newly Industrialized Economy
NIH	National Institutes of Health (U.S.)
NIST	National Institute for Standards and Technology (U.S.)
NIST	National Institute of Standards and Technology
NOAA	National Oceanic and Atmospheric Administration
NOAA	National Oceanographic and Atmospheric Administration (U.S.)
NRC	Nuclear Regulatory Commission
NSB	National Science Board
NSF	National Science Foundation
OECD	Organisation for Economic Co-operation and Development
OMB	Office of Management and Budget (U.S.)
OSTIN	Overseas Science and Technology Information Network (Korea)
PICES	North Pacific Marine Science Organization

R&D	Research and Development
RaDiUS®	Research and Development in the United States
S&E	Science and Engineering
S&T	Science and Technology
SRC	Science Research Center
STA	Science and Technology Agreement
USDA	Department of Agriculture (U.S.)
WCRP	World Climate Research Program

1. Introduction: Korean-U.S. S&T Cooperation in Context

Over the past decade, three significant shifts have changed the context of the science and technology (S&T) relationship between Korea and the United States. One is specific to the relationship: Korea has emerged into the global community as a scientifically advanced country, changing the dynamic between the two partners, putting them on a more equal footing. The second is a broader shift affecting both countries: Information and communications technologies, ease of travel, and enhanced global capacity have greatly increased the scale, scope, and network of international linkages in S&T. The third is the increased attention to global problems and issues that require input from the S&T community, including global climate change, demographic shifts, and infectious disease prevention.

The bilateral S&T policies between Korea and the United States were forged in circumstances where Korea was a "junior" partner in science, where the motivating factor for cooperation was as much political as it was scientific, and where the international network was not the dominant superstructure for science. Given the shifts in the operating environment, a critical examination of the Korean-U.S. S&T relationship stands to benefit both countries. Issues such as the potential for continued growth of the bilateral relationship, reorganization of existing programs, new areas for research emphasis, and joint outreach to third parties are points for consideration. In order to inform this review, this report describes the current S&T relationship between the Republic of Korea (Korea) and the United States. It presents information about how the two countries could enhance the S&T relationship, as well as ways in which the two countries could work together to seek additional partners. It also discusses policy options that might be profitably considered by both governments.

This report has four sections. Following this introduction, which seeks to place the Korean-U.S. relationship within the global context and present data about the relationship, Section 2 describes the institutional structures within the U.S. government and within the Korean government that support international S&T cooperation. Section 3 discusses the views of scientists participating in Korean-U.S. international collaborations. Section 4 presents analysis of opportunities for enhanced cooperation between the two parties within four modes of cooperation, as well as conclusions, policy recommendations, and suggestions for future research. Appendixes include a reprint of the RAND index of S&T capacity, the list of questions we used to guide discussions with scientists, and a list of U.S. government S&T agencies with contact information. A list of references and additional reading is also included.

Korea's Enhanced Science and Technology Capacity

S&T collaboration between Korea and the United States has grown over the past decade. Part of this increase derives from Korea's significant commitment to increase its S&T capacity. During the 1990s, Korean public and private sectors increased research and development (R&D) spending from $4.8 billion in 1991 to $11 billion in 2000 (in constant value) to account for 3 percent of its national gross domestic product (OECD, 2001). In a study conducted for the World Bank, RAND found that Korea's S&T capacity places it as number 11 among the 25 scientifically advanced countries of the world (Wagner et al., 2001, and Appendix A). The increased S&T capacity within Korea has facilitated cooperation with the United States across a broad range of sciences. In addition to greater capacity to participate in scientific collaboration, the relationship has been boosted by an historically close political relationship between Korea and the United States, forged largely in the 1950s as the result of the war on the Korean peninsula.

The Asian financial crisis (more popularly known in Korea as the "IMF Crisis") has further pushed Korea to strengthen R&D capacity and increase international R&D cooperation. The financial crisis severely shook the Korean economy and significantly reduced industry spending on R&D. However, public spending on R&D dropped only slightly and has rebounded since. The crisis hastened a major reform of Korea's S&T policies. The Special Law for Scientific and Technological Innovation was enacted in 1997 to launch a five-year plan (1997–2002) for S&T innovation. Under this plan, the public sector would increase its investment in R&D to at least 5 percent of the total government budget by the year 2002 (spending reached 4.4 percent by 2001) and public investment in basic research would rise to 20 percent of total government R&D by 2002 (spending reached 16 percent by 2000). The government also announced "Vision 2025" (or "Long-Term Vision for Science and Technology Investment Toward 2025") in September 1999 to articulate broad targets for national R&D capacity building in the near term (by year 2005: expand S&T infrastructure, increase resources, and improve relevant laws and regulations), medium term (by 2015: be major R&D promoting country in the Asia-Pacific area), and long term (by 2025: be competitive in selected S&T areas at a level comparable to G-7 countries).[1]

The 2002 World Competitiveness Yearbook produced by the International Institute for Management Development (IMD) reports that Korea has an S&T infrastructure placing them at position number 10 in the world, up from 21st place in 2001. This rating tracks closely with Korea's place on RAND's index of S&T capacity, listing Korea as number 11 among the 25 scientifically advanced countries. (IMD reports the overall competitiveness of Korea ranks them as number 27 in the world.) Similar to the RAND S&T capacity index, IMD's assessment is based on cumulative impact of gross R&D expenditure, total R&D expenditure per capita, business R&D expenditure, total R&D personnel nationwide and in business enterprise, patents granted to residents, and patent productivity. Table 1.1 summarizes the IMD data and findings.

To reach its S&T goals, the Korean government has launched several major R&D programs. These include the 21st Century Frontier R&D Program, the National Research Laboratory Program, and the Biotechnology Development Program. The 21st Century Frontier R&D Program, launched in 1999 as a follow-up to the Highly Advanced National (HAN) Project, has funded more than 20 projects at a total cost of $3.5 billion for basic and applied research in information technology, bioengineering, nanotechnology, and new materials. The National Research Laboratory Program begun in 1999 explores and fosters research centers of excellence. Up to $250,000 is awarded to a research center each year for a maximum of five years. Under this program, over 350 research centers, including 150 in academia, 90 public research institutes, and 60 in the private sector, have received funding. The number of recipients is expected to rise to 450 in 2002. The Biotechnology Development Program was launched in 2001. To date, the government has invested $270 million in genomics, proteomics, and bioinformatics research under this program.[2]

---

[1] "Science and Technology Policy," at http://www.most.go.kr/index_e.html, viewed on April 17, 2002.

[2] "National R&D Programs" at http://www.most.go.kr/index_e.html, viewed on April 17, 2002.

Table 1.1

Science Infrastructure Competitiveness of Korea

Factor	Measure	2002 Value	2002 Rank	2001 Value	2001 Rank
Total expenditure on R&D	US$ billions	122	8	100	8
Total expenditure on R&D per capita	US$ per capita	260.6	21	214.0	21
Total expenditure on R&D	Percentage of GDP	2.65	7	2.47	7
Business expenditure on R&D	US$ billions	92	6	76	10
Business expenditure on R&D per capita	US$ per capita	195.6	19	122.7	20
Total R&D personnel nationwide	Full-time work equivalent (FTE)	137.9	9	128.7	9
Total R&D personnel nationwide per capita	FTE per 1,000 people	2.96	21	2.77	21
Total R&D personnel in business enterprise	FTE	94,300	7	77,900	8
Total R&D personnel in business per capita	FTE per 1,000 people	2.01	20	1.68	19
Basic research	Basic research for long-term economic development	6.47	12	6.79	10
Science degrees	Percent of total bachelor's degrees in science and engineering	46.4	11	—	—
Scientific articles	Scientific and technical articles published by origin of author	5,411	21	—	—
Science in schools	Science in schools is adequately taught in your country	4.76	29	4.54	33
Interest in S&T	Interest in S&T is strong for the youth of your country	5.49	22	5.72	34
Nobel prizes	Awarded in physics, chemistry, physiology or medicine and economics since 1950	0	24	0	24
Nobel prizes per capita	Awarded since 1950 per million people	0	24	0	24
Patents granted to residents	Number of patents granted to residents	43,314	3	35,900	3

Table 1.1—continued

Factor	Measure	2002		2001	
		Value	Rank	Value	Rank
Change in patents granted to residents	Percentage change	20.65	13	147.64	3
Securing patents abroad	Number of patents secured abroad by country residents	7,764	10	6,501	11
Patent and copyright protection	Patent and copyright protection is adequately enforced in your country	5.82	30	6.00	32
Number of patents in force	Per 100,000 inhabitants	163	21	163	21
Patent productivity	Patents granted to residents/R&D personnel in business (000s)	515	1	—	—
Overall Rank			10		21

SOURCE: IMD (2002).

The Internationalization of Science and Technology

Korea's increased investment and rising S&T capacity have occurred as S&T overall has become more internationalized and networked. Korean government policy is an important part of the integration of its scientific community into global science. This is similar to the public policy shifts of many governments. For example, in 2000, the governments of Canada and the United States both independently issued reports on policy toward international S&T. The National Science Board (NSB) (U.S.) said, "Our participation in international S&E [science and engineering] collaborations and partnerships is increasingly important as a means of keeping abreast of important new insights and discoveries in science and engineering." The Canadian report makes similar positive statements about the role of international S&T and its contribution to the public good. In 2002, the Korean Ministry of Science and Technology (MOST) issued a report entitled "Implementation Plan for Science and Technology Internationalization Projects" that states, "By actively implementing liberalization, globalization and networking of the national S&T activities, we will take advantage of global sourcing of R&D resources effectively, and take responsibility of the international community in participating multinational S&T cooperative projects and transferring technologies to developing countries."

Governments are interested in supporting international cooperation in research and development (ICRD) for a number of reasons. Among these are efforts to increase goodwill within the international political community, to seek efficiencies involved in investing in scientific equipment, to access resources or a research location found in another country, or to work with other countries to address global problems (Wagner, 1997). Governments also see S&T as a key part of a national innovation system. Keeping active contacts with researchers in other countries is often a way to stay on top of important innovations. Some of these relationships may be re-ordered in the new security imperatives following the September 11, 2001 attacks on the United States. This re-ordering may include scrutiny of cooperation in some "dual-use" technology areas, and in genetically modified foods and other genetic projects. How this will play out in the relationship between Korea and the United States is not clear at this time.

Scientists have different reasons for taking part in collaborations. Some of them overlap with government's interests, but others do not. Reasons given by scientists for engaging in collaboration include accessing expertise, increasing the chances of receiving funds, enhancing productivity, and exposing graduate students to new research ideas (Beaver, 2000). The interests of the two parties diverge at an important point: Governments must account for the benefits of funds spent on science to national well-being, while scientists are generally interested in increasing the overall pool of knowledge and publishing their results, no matter where advances occur or benefits accrue. The fact that science is seen as contributing to national economic growth leads to some conflict over where research takes place and who benefits from it. We will discuss this topic further below.

The increase in the Korean-U.S. S&T relationship is part of a trend toward greater international collaboration overall. Recent literature suggests that knowledge creation in S&T is increasingly the result of collaboration among scientists (Smith 2000). Within the category of collaborative research, and increasing faster overall, are international linkages in scientific research (Glänzel, 2001b; Doré et al., 1996; Georghiou, 1998; Luukkonen et al., 1992; Schubert and Braun, 1990). Data collected by the NSB show that coauthored articles rose by 8 percent between 1987 and 1997 to account for 50 percent of all articles published by the latter date. During the same time, *internationally coauthored articles* doubled to account for 15 percent of all world articles (NSB, 2000). A recent article by W. Glänzel (2001b) highlights the increases in international collaboration. Figures 1.1 and 1.2 demonstrate the increase by comparing coauthorship data from 1985 and 1995. (Note the significant increase in Korean-U.S. coauthorship.)

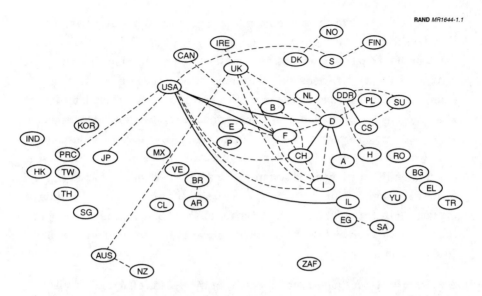

Figure 1.1—Coauthorship Maps for the 50 Most Active Countries in All Fields Combined in 1985–1986, from Wolfgang Glänzel, 2001b

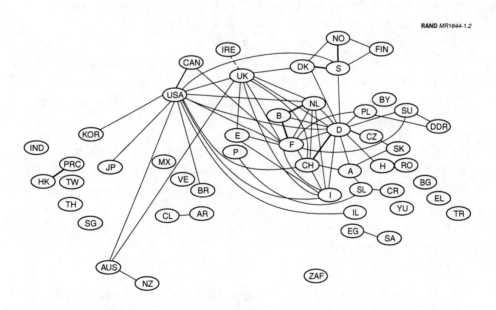

Figure 1.2—Coauthorship Maps for the 50 Most Active Countries in All Fields Combined in 1995–1996, from Wolfgang Glänzel, 2001b

A review of these data and other indicators suggests that international coauthorships have been growing over the past 20 years. There are, of course, variations in the rate of international coauthorship among countries. The average is somewhat lower for scientists in the countries with the largest scientific enterprise, most likely because opportunities are more readily available for nationally based cooperation. This is most notable for the United States, which, in 1997, produced 33.6 percent of articles in the sciences, but whose international coauthorship rate was just 18 percent (NSB, 2000). On the other end of the scale among scientifically advanced countries are the Netherlands at 36 percent, and Switzerland and Belgium both at 46 percent. Korea's rate falls in the middle of the field with 28 percent international coauthorship. (Scientifically developing countries have even higher rates of international coauthorship, regularly in the 50–60 percentile range.)

A number of reasons have been proffered for the rise in collaboration among scientists. These include the need to access facilities or resources, to gain experience, to increase the efficiency of the research process, or to work with a skilled colleague (Beaver and Rosen, 1978). The relative ease of international travel, the increasing availability of information and communications technologies (ICT), the specialization of many aspects of scientific inquiry, and the global nature of some problems facing both the scientific and policy worlds also serve to encourage cooperation (Wagner, 2001). International collaboration may also be the outgrowth of opportunity, since, over the past 20 years, many countries have increased capacity to conduct world-class research.

Linkages are increasing, not just across political borders, but among university and corporate researchers as well. The phenomenon of these cross-sectoral linkages has been described as a "triple helix" of interactions, increasing the dynamism of knowledge creation (Leydesdorff, 2000). Layered on top of the triple helix is transnational cooperation, which is an increasing feature of many, if not most, disciplines of S&T.

Patterns of Korean-U.S. Cooperation in Science and Technology

The increase in cooperation between Korea and the United States might be expected, given Korea's increasing investment in S&T. Nevertheless, the rate of increase has been higher than one would expect if just the rate of investment were taken into account. The reasons for this increase include political decisions on the part of both governments to encourage increased cooperation, as well as the enhanced capacity of Korean scientists to participate in world-class science.

The political and cultural ties between the two countries have facilitated this close relationship, but it is maintained by excellence in science.

The percentage of coauthorships cited by U.S. scientists with South Korean collaborators is less than 3 percent of all U.S. coauthorships, in contrast to 12 percent with the United Kingdom and Canada, and 8 percent with Japan. This suggests that growth in S&T cooperation may be possible between the United States and Korea. In contrast, when Korean scientists collaborate internationally, they are highly likely to coauthor with U.S. partners. The strikingly high figure of more than 60 percent of Korean coauthorships being with the United States needs further examination. In order to understand the existing scientific relationship, it is useful to understand the strengths of both parties. The following subsection discusses the S&T strengths of both parties.

Fields of Strength

Korea's strengths in global science are considerable, offering opportunities for partnerships. Korean scientists published close to 2,000 articles in international journals in 1998. This represents about 8 percent of all articles published in international scientific journals,[3] an increase from less than 1 percent in 1986 (NSB, 2000). Korean scientists are most likely to publish in international scientific journals in the fields of physics and chemistry. Figure 1.3 shows the significant growth in publications since 1988 in many fields of science, led by an increase in physics and chemistry.

Despite these strengths, Korea has an investment and publication structure similar to that of other scientifically proficient countries rather than the scientifically advanced countries. (See Appendix A for an explanation of the scientifically advanced and proficient countries index.) A bibliometric review of areas of scientific strength suggests that the scientifically advanced countries are publishing more frequently in the biological and medical sciences, moving slowly away from the physical and chemical sciences (Okubo et al., 1992). Scientifically proficient countries (which are also ones that are building an industrial base) are publishing more frequently in the physical and chemical sciences. In addition, scientifically proficient countries are more likely to maintain a close relationship with a single scientifically advanced country, while the advanced countries have varied and diverse collaborative relationships.

---

[3]The list of international journals is maintained by the Institute for Scientific Information in the United States.

10

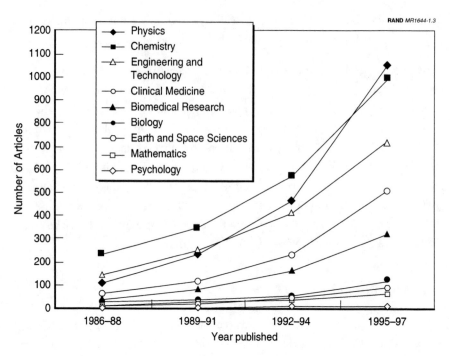

SOURCE: NSB, 2000.

Figure 1.3—Number of Scientific and Technical Articles Published by Korean Practitioners, 1986–1997

An analysis of the fields in which Korean papers are both published and cited shows that Korea maintains a specialization in physics and chemistry. Figure 1.4 illustrates shifts in Korean specialization over a ten-year period from a highly specialized position in chemistry toward a shared specialization in physics, chemistry, and engineering. The biological and biomedical sciences show room for growth.

In comparison, U.S. strengths in S&T have been shifting toward the biomedical sciences over the past ten years, although, overall, it has a balance among specializations, with a slight deficit in chemistry. Figure 1.5 illustrates a slight shift away from biology and engineering and toward biomedical research and earth and space sciences. The two countries have greatest commonality in emphases in clinical medicine and engineering. They have complementarities in chemistry, where Korea is strong and the United States does not have a highly specialized emphasis, and in physics, where Korean capacity has grown while the United States has slightly reduced its specialization. The two countries have a disconnect around the earth and space sciences and biological sciences, where U.S. specialization is growing, while Korea has no apparent specialization in either.

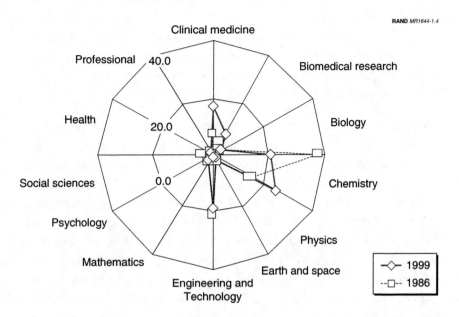

SOURCE: NSB, 2002.

Figure 1.4—Shifts in Korean Specialization Between 1986 and 1999

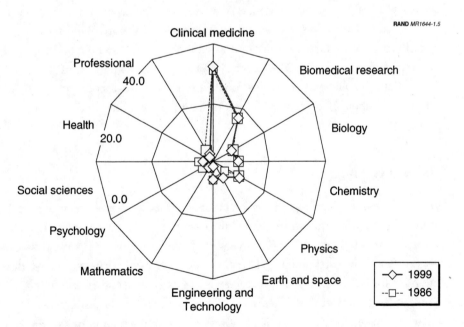

SOURCE: NSB, 2002.

Figure 1.5—Shifts in U.S. Specialization Between 1986 and 1999

A review of the projects funded by the U.S.-Korea Cooperative Science Program since 1993 shows that the fields of science most likely to be funded are in the physical, chemical and engineering sciences by a factor of 5 to 1. This reflects the fact that Korean scientists have capabilities that are compatible with U.S. partners, but it also suggests that some areas of science are not the subject of robust cooperation between Korea and the United States.

Figure 1.3 shows an increase in the percentage of Korean publications in biomedical science. This is an encouraging sign that Korean capacities are expanding beyond physics, chemistry and engineering. Nevertheless, the percentage of internationally coauthored articles in Figure 1.6 does not reflect the strengths demonstrated in the national-based citation and publication patterns: The share of these articles is declining relative to other fields. Moreover, even though Korea shows strength in physics and chemistry, these appear to be among the lowest of the fields in which Korea is copublishing with international colleagues. In an independent study, M. J. Kim constructed a field-by-field profile of Korean international publishing in the period 1994–1996. Notably, he found that 29 percent (1,042) of the papers coauthored by Koreans with researchers from other countries were in physics, the most productive field in terms of coauthorships, according to Kim. Of these papers, 32 percent were coauthored with U.S.-based scientists or engineers (Kim, 1999). Physics articles coauthored by Korean researchers with foreign researchers involved partners from 18 countries, and 93 papers coauthored with U.S. researchers had the highest citation rates (Kim, 2000). Kim (1999) found that 84 percent of internationally collaborative papers come from Korean researchers at universities, about 10 percent from government-run institutes, and about 6 percent from industry.

University Linkages

The strength of the Korean-U.S. S&T relationship has developed in large part due to the network of relationships formed through the participation of Korean students and scholars in the U.S. university system. The flow of people has been largely "one-way": very few U.S. students study in Korea, perhaps because the incentive for U.S. citizens to learn Korean is not as great as the incentive for Koreans (and many others) to learn English. Due in part to the close political alliance between the two countries that was forged in the second half of the 20th century, and the sheer size of the U.S. science system, when studying overseas, Korean students choose overwhelmingly to study in the United States. Many

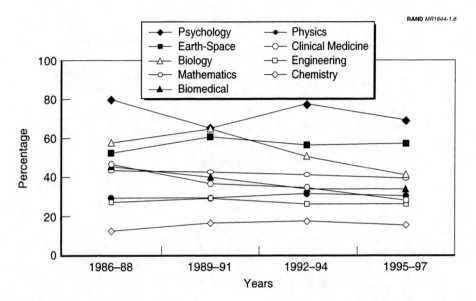

RAND MR1644-1.6

SOURCE: NSB, 2000.

Figure 1.6—S&T Articles: Percentage of Korean Articles Internationally Coauthored, by Field, 1986–1997

scientists and engineers who work in Korean universities, private industry, and national laboratories received some part of their training in the United States. Many of these practitioners retain a relationship with U.S. colleagues over the years, often returning to the United States on sabbatical or as a visiting scholar. Tables 1.2, 1.3, and 1.4 contain data on Korean students studying in the United States.

In addition to the exchange of students, there are several institutional linkages of note. The most prominent is the KIMM-MIT cooperative agreement that we will describe in more detail below.

Table 1.2

Korean Students Studying in the United States, 1987 and 1997

Year	Total Korean Students	Korean Graduate Students
1987–1988	20,520	14,939
1997–1998	42,890	18,961

SOURCE: NSB, 2002, table 2-21.

Table 1.3

Percentages of Korean Graduate Students Studying in the United States by Field, 1987 and 1997

	1987–1988	1997–1998
S&E	67.3	54.1
Social sciences	15.9	10.2
Physical & life sciences	14.5	9.0
Mathematics & computer sciences	8.8	6.9
Agriculture	2.9	2.2
Engineering	21.1	18
Other sciences	4.1	7.8
Non-S&E	32.7	45.9

SOURCE: NSB, 2002, table 2-21.

Table 1.4

Korean S&E Doctoral Recipients from U.S. Universities Who Plan to Stay in the United States

Year	Total Ph.D. Recipients	Plan to Stay (%)	Firm Plans to Stay (%)
1990	971	31.6	23.3
1991	1,107	35.2	22.0
1992	1,123	33.2	19.6
1993	1,118	35.2	18.0
1994	1,143	38.1	20.1
1995	1,000	38.8	21.0
1996	977	37.7	24.3
1997	842	41.1	29.2
1998	786	51.1	32.1
1999	738	62.7	40.2

SOURCE: NSB, 2002, table 2-32.

Government Spending on Cooperation

It is useful for our analysis to view Korean and U.S. government commitments to international cooperation in comparison to those made by other governments. However, reports on S&T spending (such as reports published by the Organisation for Economic Co-operation and Development (OECD) and the NSB) do not include data on government investment in international collaboration in R&D. Table 1.5 lists the 12 countries appearing at the top of RAND's index of scientific capacity. (See Appendix A.) Where available, the data show total R&D spending and the subset of this amount financed by government for each country listed.

From both published and unpublished sources, RAND has collected the best available estimate of how much each of these countries spends on ICRD. The figures presented are official funds *dedicated to* ICRD. However, governments also fund R&D through their regular science programs. We call these funds *spent on* ICRD. This distinction between dedicated and spent funds can be defined as follows, and it is illustrated in Figure 1.7:

- *Funds dedicated to ICRD* are those that are committed in the federal budget to support ICRD programs. They include activities such as the John Fogarty Center at the National Institutes of Health (NIH), Canada's National Resources Canada program to support international agricultural research, Japan's International Cooperative Research Project within the Science and Technology Agreement (STA), and Korea's International Science and Technology Centers. This category includes the funding of transnational programs or institutions where the pooling of national resources for a common purpose creates a supranational facility or staff. Because these funds are visible within an official budget they might be considered the "tip of the iceberg," as suggested in Figure 1.7.

- *Funds spent on ICRD* are those that emerge from research activities where scientists link with their counterparts in the course of conducting research. These activities form the bulk of collaborative R&D activities between scientifically advanced countries. This category includes the grant-based activities of hundreds of scientists, as well as training programs for doctoral students and post-doctoral fellows. These activities might be considered "the bulk of the iceberg," as illustrated in Figure 1.7. Although most governments

Table 1.5

Comparisons of Investment in International Cooperation in Research and Development, Latest Year Available

Country	Position on Capacity Index	Total National R&D Spending, All Sector, 2000 $M	Official Government Budget Dedicated to R&D, 1999 $M	Official Government Budget for ICRD, 1998 (est.) $M	Percentage of National Articles That Are Internationally Coauthored
United States	1	243,500	72,000	205	18
Japan	2	133,034	25,676	70	15
Germany	3	50,376	17,027	219	34
Canada	4	10,080	3,145	46	31
Taiwan	5	1,730	1,250	NA	18
Sweden	6	7	2	NA	39
United Kingdom	7	25,196	7,836	20	29
France	8	30,439	12,237	64	36
Switzerland	9	6	2	NA	48
Israel	10	10	3	2	38
South Korea	11	9,523	2,180		28
Finland	12	4,013	1,204		36
Notes and Sources:	RAND (2001)	OECD (2000); Table 1, figured using 1999 avg. exc. rate Taiwan and Israel from government publications	OECD (2000); percentage of GERD financed by government, 1999 or latest available; Taiwan and Israel from government publications	Includes fellowship and study grants; not including Official Development Assistance; NA = not available	NSB (2000)

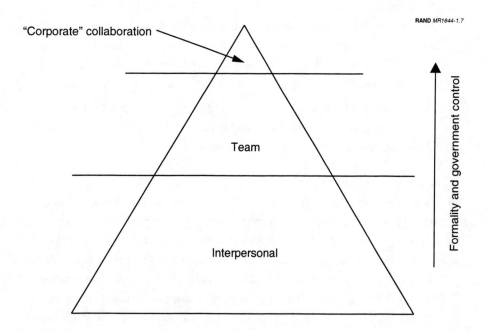

RAND *MR1644-1.7*

"Corporate" collaboration

Team

Interpersonal

Formality and government control

Figure 1.7—Illustrating the Distinction Between Corporate and Other Types of ICRD

do not budget for these activities in a way that would allow us to show "hard numbers," we have derived an estimate of this amount for each government as a way to compare countries, shown in Table 1.5.

In order to understand how much of the research enterprise is available to policymakers seeking to enhance cooperation, we need to consider the different types of cooperative relationships. David Smith and J. Sylvan Katz (2000) make a useful distinction between types of collaboration. They describe three models of collaboration—corporate partnership, team, and interpersonal —as a way to differentiate between level, rationale, structure, ownership and benefits of collaboration. (These distinctions will be important when we discuss options for enhanced collaboration in Section 4.) The three models are described as follows:

•   Corporate partnerships are highly formal, "means to an end" collaborations that are initiated by more than one group and have access to external resources as a goal.

- Team collaborations exist below the corporate model in the Smith and Katz formulation. They have a formalized existence but are not defined as formal partnerships. A motivating factor for these collaborations is the need for multidisciplinary skills and experience. This concept is similar to the Gibbons' Mode 2 concept of multidisciplinary, team-based research.

- Interpersonal collaboration is a diverse category with activities dependent upon the personal relationships between researchers or research groups. These activities are ongoing and informal.

Applying the Smith and Katz formulation to the data in Table 1.5, the column detailing the Official Government *Budget for ICRD* would be analogous to the Smith and Katz "corporate partnerships." These formal programs are formulated with specific goals of achieving complementarity or of pooling or accessing resources. The motivating factors for governments to participate often include political goals of improving relationships with specific countries, or creating goodwill and strong ties with various nations. Examples of these activities include both equipment-based programs such as Center for European Nuclear Research (CERN) and distributed research activities such as the Human Frontier Science Program. Another example is Korean and U.S. participation in the North Pacific Marine Science Organization (PICES), which was established in 1992 to promote and coordinate marine research.

Table 1.5 does not include funds spent on collaboration. To date, only the U.S. government has estimated the amount spent on team collaboration, this through studies conducted by RAND described below. Where corporate collaborations are often "top down"—government officials establish and oversee the activities—team collaborations are more often "bottom up"—scientists choose partners and apply to government for research support based on the strength of the partnership. Bottom-up activities include projects such as 2001 multinational workshops leading to the creation of a "Materials World-Net" in which Korea and the United States participated.

Extrapolating from the U.S. experience, it can be postulated that team and interpersonal collaborations account for a much larger amount of spending than is dedicated to ICRD in formal programs. The U.S. government–funded team collaboration is perhaps 20 times as high as official collaboration. Our research suggests that this ratio is similar in other governments.

Table 1.5 also does not include a column estimating the amount of spending on interpersonal collaborations. It would be difficult to attach a monetary figure to these types of exchanges. If one were to attempt a monetary estimate, it can be assumed to be an even larger amount and a more robust set of interactions than corporate or team collaborations. Scientists and policy analysts often point to the existence of "invisible colleges" of collaboration among scientists—linkages that transcend national boundaries and represent an international network of connections. Any quantitative data would understate or distort the extent of interpersonal collaborations that occur among scientists.

The different types of collaboration described above help us understand the formality of linkages and therefore the extent of government control over spending on international collaboration. However, the description does not explain why governments are interested in funding these activities. In order to understand this, we need to put R&D spending into context. The following paragraphs address this question.

Within the national budgets of the scientifically advanced countries, R&D spending can be characterized in three broadly illustrative (but not exclusive) categories: policy directed, mission focused, and science oriented.

- Policy-directed projects are those activities funded by governments where science or technology can help reach a political goal. Examples of these types of activities are funds provided to build scientific capacity in developing countries, funds dedicated to fighting the spread of infectious disease, weapons disposal, and environmental cleanup.

- Mission-oriented research is commissioned and conducted to help a government agency reach a specific goal. For example, in many scientifically advanced countries energy ministries fund research into solar energy technology in an effort to serve the mission of finding economic and environmentally sustainable sources of energy. Similarly, aeronautics agencies fund projects related to understanding and exploring space. A mission focus does not mean that the research is not *basic* research: In many cases, mission agencies fund basic research to help understand the natural world as it relates to a specific question or goal. The U.S. Department of Energy (DoE), for example, funds basic research on the chemical properties of materials that may help build photovoltaic cells. Similarly, a mission focus does not mean that the science being funded has not been reviewed for quality. In many cases, mission-focused science is peer reviewed and grants or contracts are issued on a competitive basis.

- Science-focused projects are those funded by government to support inquiries into a basic understanding of the natural world. Governments fund this type of research for a number of reasons, often noting that creation of the pool of knowledge is a public good. Funding is often provided to the

20

individual researcher or a team of researchers. At times, governments provide science-focused funds to a laboratory director for allocation to among departments of researchers.

Figure 1.8 illustrates the types of policies that coalesce into the joint activities supporting international S&T. The top-down arrows represent funds dedicated to international cooperation, as well as policy statements supporting these activities. Policy-directed cooperation and collaboration include "megascience projects" such as the International Space Station (ISS), CERN, and other equipment-based activities where governments make an explicit commitment to fund international cooperation. Also included here are the activities that governments undertake using science to address a political problem. Examples of these activities could be efforts to dismantle nuclear weapons in the former Soviet Union.

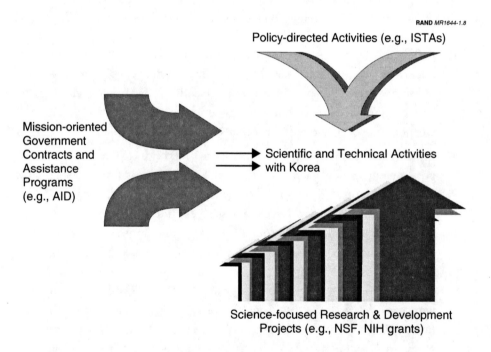

Figure 1.8—Diverse Policy Goals Influence International Cooperation in
Science and Technology

The "side on" arrows represent the mission-oriented research activities funded by agencies and ministries of government. These activities can be both policy directed (the top-down arrows) such as foreign aid for development, and science driven (the bottom-up arrows) such as energy research. These activities can also be split between funds dedicated to, and those spent on international cooperation in, S&T. For example, energy agencies may commit money to an international fusion project as part of their overall mission. This would be a contribution to *dedicated* international activities.

The bottom-up arrows are those science-oriented activities that governments fund, often through grants to individual scientists, to increase the overall pool of knowledge. These projects may have international cooperative and collaborative linkages, but the associations that emerge arise from the interests of the investigators and practitioners. These activities are "below the water line"—they are funds *spent on* international collaboration.

Within the scope of these three categories of R&D funding, the choice by program managers of where research takes place falls into two broad categories: outside of government ("extramural") or inside government labs ("intramural"). Extramural research is that set of government grants, contracts, and cooperative agreements that are conducted in the university and private-sector laboratories. In the United States, for example, more than 70 percent of government-funded R&D takes place outside of government laboratories—in other words, it is extramural research. Intramural research is that part of the government's R&D budget that takes place within government laboratories. In France and Germany, much more research takes place within government laboratories, and the percent of intramural research is higher than it is in the United States.

Cooperation in intramural research, because it is often tied to the laboratory, takes place within the national borders of the country funding that research. For example, a researcher from Europe may visit a DoE laboratory in the United States in order to work on a project. Cooperation in extramural research can also be collocated in central research facilities, but it is more likely than intramural science to be *distributed*. In distributed research, practitioners work on a common research project, but each works out of his or her home lab and shares research results using the Internet and other forms of communications. RAND research suggests that distributed collaboration is growing as a share of all international science.

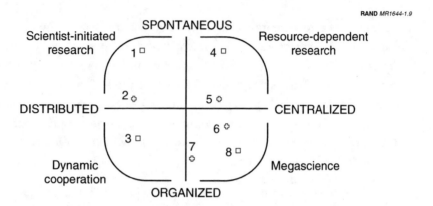

1. Investigation into Material Formability; 2. Cross-Language Information Retrieval Planning Project; 3. U.S.-Korea Workshop on New Frontiers in Infrastructural and Seismic Engineering; 4. Climate Research; 5. Ocean Research; 6. CERN; 7. ISS; 8. ITER

Figure 1.9—Organization of Cooperation with Examples of Korean-U.S. Activities

In addition to describing and discussing types of collaboration, there appear to be a number of *motivating factors* behind the organization of collaboration that can also be discussed using Figure 1.9. Crawford, Shinn, and Sörlin (1993) were among the first to suggest that space and earth sciences were "out front" in populating international science because the subjects are based upon resources that transcend national boundaries. In these cases, researchers travel to different geographical locations in order to access key *resources* needed to observe and experiment. Arctic research, earthquake research, and investigations into climate change are examples of this type of resource-based collaboration. These have characteristics of *spontaneous-centralized* research, located in the top right quadrant of Figure 1.9.

Another factor motivating organizational linkages in international collaboration is the location of key *data sources* needed for research. In some cases, one research institute or group of scientists has compiled a database of or has access to key information that can be useful to other researchers. In such cases, researchers often need to work with the originators of the data in order to complete their research. Medical research reporting on longitudinal data over a large demographic area is one example of this type of research. Biological systems research involving a unique data set, such as the mosses of northern China, is another example. These types of research projects might logically fall into the *organized-distributed* quadrant of Figure 1.9.

A third motivating factor for international linkages is the well-known phenomenon of gathering scientists around a piece of equipment. Usually the equipment is of such a scale that no one country can afford to pay for it alone. As a result, several nations join forces to pay for the equipment with the understanding that their scientists will have preferential access to the equipment. This type of research activity has been called "megascience" because of the scale of the investment. These activities are among those projects that can be considered *organized-centralized*, and so would fall into the bottom right quadrant of Figure 1.9. High-energy physics, space exploration, and astronomy are examples of researchers sharing large equipment on an international basis.

A fourth motivating factor for international linkages is interpersonal communications arising from professional interactions. These types of collaborative linkages arise among scientists who learn about each other's work through cooperative information exchange. Often scientists meet at professional conferences and learn that they have common research interests. At other times, researchers may read publications that inspire them to contact each other. They communicate with each other from within their own laboratories. At times, they find reasons (sometimes the reasons cited above) to collaborate. The collaborations that arise out of these interactions are the ones that would fall into the *spontaneous-distributed* quadrant in Figure 1.9. We will return to these features of policy and motivating factors below when we discuss options for enhancing the Korean-U.S. relationship.

In summary, funds for scientific research emerge from within the political process to serve a number of goals. Some of these goals include international exchanges on a formal or "corporate partnership" level, and some emerge from the goals of scientists and form at the team or interpersonal level. Funds for international science include those that are explicitly dedicated to international science as a tool of government to serve foreign policy and scientific goals, as well as those that are spent on international S&T to serve missions and fund science. Collaborative research can take place within government laboratories, in shared facilities such as internationally funded laboratories or research centers, or at distributed locations in universities or industry. The linkages established between scientists from different countries create proposals and articles that can (imperfectly) measure a network called "international science." Different motivating factors and organizational imperatives are attached to these different types of cooperation, all of which affect the funding, management, and eventual outcomes of research.

Corporate Linkages Are Increasing

Although influenced by different factors than those affecting government spending, research shows that corporate cooperation in R&D, as well as investments in foreign research centers, is increasing sharply throughout the industrialized world. International business alliances in research are up more than eight-fold since the mid-1980s. In the late 1980s, and continuing into the 1990s, joint non-equity R&D agreements were the most important form of partnership among private-sector companies. The formation of these strategic technology partnerships has been particularly extensive among high technology firms in ICT, biotechnology, and new materials. Total alliances in these three fields increased from 120 in 1980 to close to 500 in 1996 (Jankowski, 1998).

There are many reasons why firms invest in research partnerships with foreign companies or in a foreign country, but, as John Jankowski (1998) notes, "all relate to growth in global innovation and the strategic need to establish networks for creating and strengthening firm-specific technological capabilities." Foreign companies now invest significantly more in R&D than they did in the past, a trend that is improving opportunities for linkages across national borders.

Technology has been one of the major driving forces of rapidly growing international strategic alliances. Kang and Sakai (2000) describe three mechanisms that facilitate and motivate these alliances:

- Information and communications technologies such as the Internet, e-mail, and electronic data interchange (EDI) enable firms to carry out research in different locations concurrently.
- Multiplying research costs accompanied by shorter product life cycles prompts the sharing of resources and risks internationally, especially in ICT.
- R&D alliances in developing global standards are particularly sought between technology inventors and leading multinationals with global brand name and marketing power.

Korea and the United States have been active participants in global strategic alliances. In contrast to the practices of other Asian countries (where labs have been established on home soil), Korean companies actively established R&D laboratories in the United States. Korean companies more than doubled the number of their R&D facilities in the United States from about a dozen in 1992 to 32 in 1998 (22 for ICT and electronics, 3 for biotech and chemicals, 4 for automotive, and 1 for consumer goods), ranking sixth as an active research partner in the United States (Dalton et al., 1999). In a review of this practice,

Amsden et al. (2001) noted that Korean companies conducting R&D overseas closely tie it to production, thus enhancing overall productivity. Compared to the R&D investment inflow from overseas to Korea, the Korean R&D investment outflow from Korea is much bigger ($502 million in 1998 and $433 million in 1999, see Table 2.4). The majority of overseas Korean R&D expenditures has been made by Korean business (as opposed to government)—$469 million in 1998—accounting for 6.8 percent of the total R&D spending committed within the private sector.

Within Korea, foreign companies have not been particularly active in R&D investment in the 1980s, but the situation began to change in the 1990s. For example, Motorola built its first plants in Korea in 1967. These were manufacturing facilities that conducted little R&D activity. In 1996, Motorola established its first semiconductor laboratory in Korea and this was followed by a software center in 1997. The two facilities together employ about 200 Korean scientists.

Between 1997 and 1999, foreign direct investment in Korea grew from $6.9 billion to $15.5 billion. Although there are no official statistics on international industrial R&D cooperation in Korea, Kim et al. (2000) surveyed 147 companies, including 48 U.S. companies, and found that the average ratio of R&D expense to total sales volume is 3.5 percent and the ratio of research personnel to total employees exceeds 10 percent. The Korean Ministry of Finance also found that foreign companies have increased their emphasis on new-product development. Many, in particular, appreciate the "triple helix" value of Korean universities and research institutes as potential R&D partners. According to the U.S. Department of Commerce (DoC) (1998), U.S. companies invest nearly $15 billion per year in offshore R&D, roughly 10 percent of their total R&D budgets. According to Richard Florida (1998), "Foreign-owned laboratories are a response in part to the rapid and thoroughgoing globalization of markets—in particular the fact that goods are increasingly produced where they are sold." International alliances, cross-national investment in R&D, and the investment by multinationals in building foreign labs enable a great deal more direct access to foreign S&T know-how than has ever been the case in the past.

U.S. companies have increased their overall R&D spending abroad from $5.2 billion in 1987 to $14.2 billion in 1997, and this represents 11 percent of U.S. R&D expenditures. Five countries, Germany, the United Kingdom, Canada, France, and Japan, account for more than half of the U.S. R&D expenditures abroad, and recently R&D spending by U.S. firms in some newly industrializing countries, including Singapore, Brazil, China, and Mexico, has increased. U.S. R&D expenditures in Korea tripled from $14 million in 1992 to $42 million in 1997, but are still lower than U.S. investment in other Asian newly industrialized economies (NIEs): Taiwan ($87 million), Hong Kong ($84 million), and Singapore ($73 million) (NSB, 2000).

One indicator of the strength of industrial R&D activities is the registering of foreign patents. The United States is one of the largest owners of patents covering foreign inventions: The share of foreign inventions in its patent portfolio is 43 percent. The number of U.S. patents by Korean firms surged over the last decade, from 159 patents granted in 1989 to 3,562 patents granted in 1999, putting Korean firms sixth among foreign-based firms seeking patents in the United States (NSB, 2002). However, Korea is less internationalized than other scientifically advanced countries with respect to cross-border ownership of inventions: The percentage of patents with foreign coinventors is 4.8 percent for the United States and 3.9 percent for Korea, compared with 7.2 percent on average among the OECD countries.

2. Institutional Support for Cooperation

This section describes the institutions within the U.S. government and the government of Korea that support and maintain international collaboration in S&T. Much of the information on the U.S. government is drawn from an earlier RAND report, *International Cooperation in Research and Development: An Update to an Inventory of U.S. Government Spending*, MR-1248, 2001.

U.S. Government Agencies Supporting International Cooperation

The U.S. government actively supports and participates in international S&T initiatives. In 1997, the U.S. government spent more than $4.3 billion to support S&T cooperative activities, out of a federal R&D budget of $72 billion. These activities range from huge multinational megascience projects (like the International Space Station) to small grants that fund research experiments conducted by U.S. scientists in cooperation with their counterparts in other countries. It also includes assistance projects such as those helping to develop a pest-resistant strain of wheat for Central American farms, monitoring of the global atmosphere, or seeking the causes of disease. International cooperation in R&D amounts to about 6 percent of the U.S. federal R&D budget (Wagner, Yezril, and Hassell, 2001).

In addition to spending on international R&D, the government also funds other activities that have a scientific or technological component and that involve international coordination or cooperation. These activities include weather tracking, mapping, seismic detection, and space and defense operations. In 1997, mission-oriented activities accounted for perhaps as much as $1 billion of U.S. government spending over and above R&D spending.

With only a few exceptions,[4] the U.S. government does not fund international S&T activities for their own sake: Collaborative activities usually build scientific capabilities that are central to scientific or national interests or that meet mission-specific requirements. Accordingly, international activities are not budgeted

---

[4]At least two R&D agencies have offices designed to coordinate and encourage international linkages. The Fogarty Center at the National Institutes of Health spends R&D funds to facilitate international exchange, and the Office of International Programs at the National Science Foundation provides assistance to existing collaborations to aid with travel or conferencing requirements.

separately or in a manner that can be easily identified and tracked. Determining how these funds are being spent requires analysts to review descriptions of thousands of individual programs, projects, and awards and to interview government officials. Even within specific programs and projects it is often difficult to decouple international activities from other parts of the program. We estimate, based on an evaluation of project-level activities, that the U.S. government spent more than $10 million on cooperative R&D projects with Korea in FY2000.

The U.S. government policy toward international S&T cooperation is diffused among the agencies that support science. Unlike Korea, which has leadership offered by its Ministry of Science and Technology, the U.S. government does not have a single agency directing science. As a result, many policies, including ICRD, emerge from within the framework of other missions and policies. Moreover, due to the size of the U.S. R&D enterprise, attention to international linkages is not a high-priority item. U.S. research is often at the leading edge of science, and this can limit interest in cooperation. U.S.-based researchers often do not need to look too far to find collaborators. This can be frustrating for other governments looking for the U.S. policy toward "international cooperation." Moreover, in the wake of the attacks on the United States of September 11, 2001, there may be more scrutiny of collaborative research, and less interest in seeing linkages develop, particularly in fields that may transfer key or dual-use technology. The long-standing security relationship between Korea and the United States may help to buffer it from increased reticence to collaborate, but this should be a point of discussion between the two countries.

This subsection describes the role of U.S. government agencies in supporting international S&T. For each agency, an overall description of its commitment to cooperation is provided.[5] Where the information is available (either through Research and Development in the United States (RaDiUS®), the U.S. Department of State (DoS), or as a result of staff interviews), we describe projects and agreements with Korean partners. Table 2.1 provides a summary of agency commitments to cooperation.

---

[5]The reader should note that some of these findings have been reported in earlier RAND studies, including Wagner, Yezril, and Hassell, 2001. See references for a full list of relevant reports.

Table 2.1

**A Summary of U.S. Government Agency Profiles:
Commitment to ICRD and Relationship to Korea**

Agency	Intensity of commitment to ICRD (high, medium, low percentage of ICRD compared with total R&D budget)	Estimated budget dedicated to ICRD (for all countries) (FY97) ($M)	Currently has established S&T agreements with Korea? (yes, no)	Has active projects with Korea? (completed, active, planned)
Agency for International Development	low	225	no	completed
Dept. of Agriculture	medium	10	yes	active
Dept. of Commerce	medium (NOAA and NIST)	0	yes	active
Dept. of Defense	low	260	yes	active
Dept. of Energy	medium	180	yes	active
Dept. of Health and Human Services	high	215	yes	active
Environmental Protection Agency	low	20	no	completed
National Aeronautics and Space Administration	high	3,150	yes	active
National Science Foundation	high	210	yes	active
Smithsonian Institution	medium	30	no	no

Appendix C provides detailed information (available as of spring 2002) about the offices in different agencies responsible for handling contacts relevant to international S&T cooperation. Table C.1 also contains information about the R&D budgets for fiscal year 2000 for U.S. government science agencies. Contact information is included.

Agency for International Development (AID)

AID's mission includes conducting R&D with and for the benefit of third-country partners. In FY97, the R&D funding for these activities was $225 million. AID spends the bulk of its R&D money, $140 million, on global issues such as infectious disease, disaster prevention, and environmental concerns. Spending on research with, for, or in Africa represents the bulk of AID's regional spending ($38.1 million), followed by spending in Asia and the Near East ($22 million), Latin America and the Caribbean ($2.1 million), and Europe/the Commonwealth of Independent States (CIS) ($1.9 million). AID does not break down its budget below these broad categories, nor are project descriptions available, so additional analysis of AID activities was not possible for this study. AID no longer has activities with South Korea because it is no longer considered a developing country.

Department of Agriculture (USDA)

The USDA has an extensive international program that includes ICRD activities sponsored in or with many other countries. In FY97, the USDA sponsored about $10 million in international cooperative research activities through five bureaus: the Cooperative State Research, Education and Extension Service; the Forest Service; the Foreign Agricultural Service; the Animal and Plant Health Inspection Service; and the Agricultural Research Service. The majority of USDA support took the form of grants to university-based researchers and technical support funds for international cooperative research.

When USDA projects were conducted on a binational basis, those countries that accounted for the greatest dollar amount were Mexico, Russia, New Zealand, and Israel. Projects with Korea have included (1) the East Asian Agriculture Project to gain an understanding of research, production, and marketing, and (2) uses of potential East Asian alternative crops in Asia and in the United States.

Department of Commerce (DoC)

The DoC has a comparatively modest FY97 R&D budget—$915 million—of which $41 million was devoted to some form of international cooperation activities at the National Institute for Standards and Technology (NIST) and the National Oceanic and Atmospheric Administration (NOAA). NOAA's ICRD activities account for the bulk of the DoC's spending on international cooperative activities. NOAA spent close to $36 million on ICRD in FY97. This funding contributed to joint projects and data sharing with many other countries related to global climate change research, meteorology, and marine life monitoring.

In contrast to the small amount of funds spent on ICRD, the DoC reported to the DoS the largest number of international S&T agreements—299—of any of the R&D-sponsoring agencies. These International Science and Technology Agreements (ISTAs) are memoranda of understanding (MOUs) with other countries to conduct data and personnel exchanges. Examples of ISTAs between NOAA and a Korean institution include:

- The Forecast Systems Laboratory of NOAA, the Meteorological Research Institute of the Korea Meteorological Administration, and the Systems Engineering Research Institute of the Korean Institute of Science and Technology have an MOU for technical cooperation in meteorology. The emphasis is on systems and forecasting tools directed toward improved mesoscale forecasting capabilities.

- An agreement outlining cooperation in the Global Learning and Observations to Benefit the Environment (GLOBE) program, an international environmental science and education program for K–12 students worldwide. Working under the guidance of GLOBE, trained teachers and students make environmental measurements at or near their schools, report their data through the Internet to a GLOBE data processing facility, receive global images created from worldwide GLOBE school data, and study environmental topics.

In addition, DoC ICRD spending was the most productive of any R&D agency, accounting for 33 patents from 1991 to 1996—the most of any agency examined in this study. The patents resulting from international cooperation sponsored by DoC were mainly registered by scientists from NIST.

Department of Defense (DoD)

The Department of Defense devotes a significant amount of funding to ICRD, totaling close to $260 million in FY97 (the latest year for which data are available). However, the intensity of ICRD activities is low compared with its overall R&D budget, which was $37.6 billion in FY97. The low level of DoD's ICRD intensity may be due largely to the absence of a mandate for DoD to conduct R&D jointly with other countries, in contrast to that of National Aeronautics and Space Administration or the National Science Foundation, which have clear missions to cooperate with other countries. The Department of the Air Force leads other DoD units in its commitment to international cooperation, with over $130 million in ICRD spending, followed by the Army, the Navy, and the Defense Advanced Research Projects Agency.

DoD's international cooperative activities are dominated by a number of large contracts (more than $10 million each) granted to foreign companies or research institutes to conduct R&D on large systems, such as missiles and space projects. In addition to its contracting activity, DoD laboratory-based researchers undertake joint scientific research with foreign counterparts for scores of small projects. DoD ICRD joint efforts were conducted primarily with researchers from the United Kingdom, Australia (satellite system development), Russia, Israel, and various European countries.

DoD has had considerable exchange with Korea in R&D, in part because the United States maintains a significant military presence there. Cost-sharing arrangements negotiated over the past 12 years have included cooperation in R&D. Joint projects in which the United States and Korea have cooperated are:

- The Youth Science Activities, sponsored by the Army, to fund science fairs for outstanding science students.
- The development of a hybrid learning model for sequential decisionmaking, sponsored by the Army.
- Hydrographic measurements and survey of circulation in semi-enclosed seas (the CREAM Project) in support of circulation process studies, sponsored by the Navy.
- An international symposium on the physics of semiconductors, held in Korea in 1998, sponsored by the Navy.

S&T agreements signed by DoD with Korean partners include:

- Formulation of alternate dual mode lock-on-after-launch (LOAL) guidance and terminal homing concepts for short- and medium-range air defense systems, demonstration of their feasibility, and testing their performance in simulation (with the U.S. Army).
- New underground explosives storage techniques will be developed, tested, and validated, which, when utilized, will reduce explosives storage hazards and correct current deficiencies with no reduction in security, operational readiness, or logistical support (with the U.S. Army).

Department of Energy (DoE)

DoE ICRD spending is about $180 million per year. This is a small portion of the agency's overall R&D budget, which was $5.5 billion in FY97. Within the department's programs, High Energy and Nuclear and Plasma Physics programs commit the largest amount to projects involving international cooperation with multiple partners, totaling about $20 million in FY97. This included commitments to the International Thermonuclear Experimental Reactor (ITER), a large international fusion research project.

Among DoE's contract laboratories, 13 list programs or projects that involved cooperating with foreign researchers or research institutes. Among the projects we identified at the labs, Argonne National Laboratory's research base had the largest number of projects with partners from many different nations, with co-operative research programs accounting for more than $35 million in FY97. Sandia (ICRD—$22 million), Lawrence Livermore (ICRD—$24 million), and Pacific Northwest Laboratories (ICRD—$15 million) also had significant international cooperative research activities with partners from many different nations.

DoE projects with Korea include both binational projects and joint participation in multinational projects. An example of the latter is the Fusion Energy Research for Advancing Understanding and Innovation in High-performance Plasmas that will be conducted, in part, using the Korean Superconducting Tokamak Advanced Research device under construction in Korea. The International Nuclear Energy Research Initiative (I-NERI) is a major mechanism used by DoE for bilateral collaborations, some of which involve Korean scientists. DoE's Pacific Northwest National Laboratory and KISTEP (Korean Institute of Science and Technology Evaluation and Planning) have signed an agreement focusing on advanced technologies for improving the cost, safety, and proliferation resistance of nuclear energy systems.[6]

DoE's official report to DoS on binational cooperation cites 54 international S&T agreements to conduct ICRD in effect with various countries in 1997. The agency's international office reported to RAND that DoE has more than 500 international S&T agreements active at the treaty and subtreaty level. (Unlike most other agencies, DoE has statutory authority to enter into executive level cooperative agreements, such as those supporting ICRD, without requesting ap-

---

[6]I-NERI Bilateral Collaborations, http://www.pnl.gov/ineri/korea.html, viewed on May 17, 2002.

proval from DoS.) DoE does not have a specific count of bilateral agreements with Korea.

Department of Health and Human Services (HHS)

Among the agencies of HHS, the National Institutes of Health (NIH) spends the largest amount on projects involving international collaboration and cooperation. Other HHS agencies participating in ICRD are the Centers for Disease Control (CDC) and the Agency for Health Care Policy and Research.

NIH's international cooperative programs and projects totaled more than $215 million in FY97 R&D funds. Included in this total was the FY97 R&D funding of $26.5 million for the Fogarty International Center to support a range of international cooperative research projects, conferences, and educational activities. Among the institutes, the top five ICRD spenders are the National Cancer Institute (NCI) (ICRD—$43 million), the National Institute of Allergy and Infectious Diseases (ICRD—$28 million), the National Heart, Lung, and Blood Institute (ICRD—$13.5 million), the National Institute of Neurological Disorders and Stroke (ICRD—$13 million), and the National Institute of Child Health and Human Development (ICRD—$12.7 million). These institutes were also among the top eight institutes in NIH's funding in the FY97 budget.

The ICRD spending figures for NIH do not necessarily include the amounts spent on the activities in which foreign scientists take part in NIH laboratory-based research. In recent years, NIH has hosted more than 3,000 foreign scientists per year as visitors or guest researchers to conduct research. A particular example is that of the NCI, which brought a total of 117 scientists from 32 countries to the United States in FY01 for both short-term and long-term exchange programs; of those 117 scientists, five were from Korea. In that same year, through the NIH Visiting Program, 930 foreign scientists visited NCI laboratories, 91 of whom were Korean.[7]

NIH projects that have been conducted in cooperation with Korean scientists include:

- The minority international research training program conducted at the Hormone Research Center in Korea.

- Asia-Pacific Diabetes Epidemiology Training Course to develop collaborative networks with researchers through a course held in Seoul, Korea.

---

[7]National Cancer Institute, *Summary of International Activities*, March 20, 2002, http://www.cancer.gov/about_nci/oia.

CDC spent close to $15 million of its $217 million FY95 R&D budget on international cooperative projects with many countries.[8] In addition to direct spending on ICRD, CDC provides reimbursable support to other countries on infectious diseases and epidemiology that is only partly reflected in the $15 million total. The Agency for Health Care Policy and Research also spent about $2 million on ICRD activities. These agencies did not report any cooperative projects with Korea.

Environmental Protection Agency (EPA)

EPA participates actively in the Global Climate Change project to facilitate international scientific data exchange and cooperative research. In FY97, EPA spent about $20 million on ICRD, the majority of which was dedicated to some aspect of global climate change research. EPA's Air Quality division was the primary manager for this activity. The Toxic Substances and Water Quality divisions also sponsored ICRD activities. A project was conducted with Korea in 1999 to seek control agents for harmful algal blooms.

National Aeronautics and Space Administration (NASA)

NASA leads government agencies in total ICRD dollars spent: Approximately $3.1 billion, or 20 percent of its total R&D spending, is devoted to ICRD activities. International cooperation is a charter mission of this agency. Congress funds activities such as the ISS, the Cassini Satellite Program, Mars '94, Earth Observing Satellite System, and the advanced space transportation program with the understanding that these activities will be conducted in cooperation with foreign space agencies and international entities.

The programs within NASA that have the greatest commitment to ICRD are Mission to Planet Earth, Space Science, the ISS, the Space Shuttle, and Life and Microgravity Science. The ISS represents a very large portion of NASA's R&D budget. NASA's main international partners include countries with advanced space programs: Russia, Japan, France, the United Kingdom, Germany, Canada, Brazil, and the European Space Agency.

In FY95, NASA reported 60 international agreements to DoS (Title V Report). The agreements were signed by NASA to encourage and support cooperation in S&T. When sponsoring international science endeavors, NASA's work involves the exchange of scientific data and information. When building systems and

---

[8]CDC was unable to validate FY97 numbers, so the FY95 figure is used instead.

spacecraft, NASA's collaborative activities often involve parsing out to different partners the R&D of specific components of large systems or cooperating on the accomplishment of a specific mission originating either at NASA or in a foreign space agency. NASA's partners provide specific components to NASA, and the final product is incorporated into a larger system, spacecraft, or mission. Each of the international partners expects to benefit from the scientific data generated by the cooperative efforts.

National Science Foundation (NSF)

Among the U.S. government's science agencies, NSF has by far the most varied and extensive support for projects with an international component. While the total amount of funds spent on projects featuring scientific cooperation, about $206 million, does not approach NASA or DoD levels, NSF's ICRD activities represent 10 percent of that agency's FY97 R&D spending of $2.2 billion, making NSF a highly ICRD-intensive agency.[9] Moreover, in terms of total numbers of ICRD projects, NSF exceeds most other agencies. NSF funds hundreds of small grants to researchers taking part in collaborative research, technical data exchange, or conferences with foreign researchers.

In addition to funding grants that support ICRD, NSF funds the operation of four centers serving as focal points for international research: the National Astronomy and Ionospheric Center, the National Center for Atmospheric Research, the National Optical Astronomy Observatory, and the National Radio Astronomy Observatory. These centers house researchers from around the world and provide data that support the work of scientists in dozens of countries. NSF's contribution to "big science" projects includes funding ocean drilling and polar research.

Within the NSF directorates, Geosciences leads other directorates in funding projects for international collaborative functions, awarding grants of over $28 million to international activities, an amount representing 7 percent of total R&D funds for this directorate. The Directorate for Geosciences supports large international projects such as ocean drilling, global climate change, and scores of smaller projects on earthquake sciences and seismology.

The Directorate for Social, Behavioral and Economic Sciences follows closely behind Geosciences in total commitments to projects with an international

---

[9]This amount also does not include capital investment projects that NSF has funded in other countries, nor does it include education and training moneys spent on international projects, since these expenditures are not accounted for as R&D.

component, in large part because this directorate contains the Division on International Cooperative Scientific Activities, a division of NSF with FY97 R&D spending totaling $18 million. This directorate manages the U.S.-Korea Cooperative Science Program, which seeks to increase the level of cooperation between U.S. and Korean scientists and engineers through the exchange of scientific information, ideas, skills, and techniques and through collaboration on common problems. Among the diverse research activities funded under the U.S.-Korea program are:

- A cooperative research project to determine the source of immigrant species of rice plant hoppers.
- Experimenting on computational fluid dynamics methods that can be used to assist in the design and optimization of cardiac assist devices.
- A theoretical study of dielectric response functions and applications to screening of superconducting properties of solid systems.
- Detailing the physical properties of silicon nitride ceramic systems.
- Modeling and analyzing communications behavior of parallel programs on distributed-memory multiprocessors.
- Fermotosecond spectroscopy of photosynthetic light harvesting.
- Analyzing performance characteristics of future wireless communications systems.
- Improving friction brakes by eliminating tribological problems.
- Mapping the magnetic field configuration of the sun.

In addition to these activities, the NSF Office of International Science and Engineering (formerly the Division of International Programs), has two programs to increase international awareness and collaboration with Korea. One is the Summer Institute in Korea, a program to bring U.S. science and engineering graduate students to Korea. In 2002, NSF sponsored 20 students who studied in Korea for eight weeks, working in a diverse range of laboratories under the direction of a senior Korean researcher. This program is a partnership with the Korea Science and Engineering Foundation (KOSEF). In addition, NSF participates with the American Association for the Advancement of Science to bring U.S. high school students to Korea.

Smithsonian Institution

Although not a government agency, the Smithsonian Institution received a direct appropriation of $137 million in FY97 federal government R&D funds, of which a significant portion went to support ICRD projects and the operation of laboratories for the conduct of cooperative research. In consultation with Smithsonian staff and on examination of Smithsonian's budget, we estimate that the Smithsonian committed about $30 million to ICRD in FY97. The majority of this funding was spent in the Smithsonian's science programs, specifically the Smithsonian Tropical Research Institute, located in Costa Rica, and in the International Environmental Science Program. The Smithsonian also funds an international center for R&D and maintains the Canal Zone Biological Area Fund in Panama—both centers of international scientific research. The Smithsonian has registered with DoS two executive-level agreements to conduct joint scientific activities. The Smithsonian did not report any cooperative projects with Korea.

Other U.S. Government Agencies

Smaller federal R&D agencies also conduct ICRD or share scientific data as part of their S&T programs, but their budgets for these activities are very small. These agencies include the Department of Veterans Affairs (DVA), the Department of the Interior (DoI), and the Nuclear Regulatory Commission (NRC). For example, in FY97, DVA sponsored about $6.7 million of research with some international linkages. A DVA project with Korea focused on the molecular mechanisms by which cells detect and respond to extracellular signals, and another focused on comparing U.S. and Korean data on the incidence of gastric cancer.

Korean Agencies Supporting International Collaboration

Korea actively supports ICRD and seeks opportunities to participate in binational and multinational R&D projects. The Korean government reports that the total government R&D budget related to S&T international cooperation was 45.5 billion won ($37.7 million) in 1998, 41.5 billion won ($36.2 million) in 1999, and 44.8 billion won ($35.6 million) in 2000, accounting for 1.7 percent, 1.4 percent, and 1.3 percent of the R&D budget respectively. These percentage shares for *formal* collaboration are similar to those of other countries. These funds are the "tip of the iceberg" illustrated in Figure 1.7. We estimate that total spending on ICRD (corporate, team, and interpersonal collaborations) may be in the range of $800 million, an estimate drawn from examining Korean R&D spending in relation to the rate of international coauthorships.

Interest in ICRD arises out of an R&D system that has been growing rapidly over the past 15 years. R&D investment in Korea has increased throughout the 1990s as shown in Table 2.2, and the ratio of R&D to gross domestic product (GDP) has increased as well. In the 1990s, R&D investment tripled from 4.2 billion won ($4.8 million) in 1991 to 12 billion won ($9.3 million) in 1999 in nominal value, and more than doubled in real value. The private sector is responsible for the greater percentage of Korean R&D investment, followed by public sources: The ratio of public to private sources of R&D expenditure was 25 to 75 in 2000. Foreign sources have not been a substantial part of the investment.

The Korean government established a national R&D funding mechanism in the 1980s to expedite industrial restructuring, and then, in the 1990s, public R&D expanded to encourage collaborative R&D among industry, universities, and government-supported research institutes (GRIs). Table 2.3 shows the historical development of national R&D programs by various ministries since the National R&D Program was established by MOST in 1982. In 1992, The HAN Project, a large-scale R&D project with funding from government and industry, was designed and launched as a ten-year interministerial program. The HAN Project aimed to develop future-oriented technologies, such as an Integrated Services

Table 2.2

Trends of R&D Expenditures in Korea, by Source of Funds

Year	Total R&D Expenditures (current price in billion won)	Total R&D Expenditures (constant price in billion won)[a]	Total R&D Expenditures (in US$ million)[b]	As a Percent of GDP	Share of the Total R&D Expenditure		
					Gov.-Public Source	Private Source	Foreign Source
1991	4,158	6,005	4,767	1.92%	19.4%	80.4%	0.18%
1992	4,989	6,689	5,310	2.03%	17.2%	82.4%	0.43%
1993	6,153	7,707	6,118	2.22%	16.7%	83.1%	0.20%
1994	7,895	9,189	7,295	2.44%	15.9%	84.0%	0.04%
1995	9,441	10,252	8,139	2.50%	18.9%	81.1%	0.01%
1996	10,878	11,370	9,026	2.60%	22.0%	77.8%	0.13%
1997	12,186	12,345	9,800	2.69%	23.4%	76.5%	0.10%
1998	11,337	10,934	8,680	2.55%	26.9%	73.0%	0.07%
1999	11,922	11,738	9,318	2.47%	26.9%	73.1%	0.06%
2000	13,849	13,849	10,993	2.68%	24.9%	75.0%	0.07%

SOURCE: MOST evaluation, 2001.

[a]Estimated with the price level of 2000 as a base year.

[b]US$ value is estimated as constant price/exchange rate in 2000, 1,260 won/$, to avoid the distortions caused by changes in inflation and especially exchange rate (e.g., 844 won/$ in 1996 and 1,415 won/$ in 1997).

Digital Network (ISDN), next-generation automobiles, a thin-film transistor liquid crystal display (TFT-LCD), advanced materials for technologies, an advanced manufacturing system, environmental technology, and a next-generation nuclear reactor.

Based on the perceived success of the HAN Project, in 1999 the Korean government initiated the 21st Century Frontier R&D Program. Conceived as a combination of basic and applied research, the program has a greater focus than earlier efforts on emerging technologies such as biotechnology, information technology, nanotechnology, and aeronautics. The Korean government plans to support a total of 20 projects with targets in intelligence systems research, bioengineering, nanotechnology, new materials, and environmental technologies. Each project is slated to last ten years and is expected to receive about $8 million annually. The 21st Century Frontier Program has a new management system in which a project manager will be in control of each project and be given discretion to allocate resources. These projects will actively seek foreign participation. MOST officials plan to evaluate each project every three years on the basis of "visible, clear, and quantitative" evidence (quantifiable objective and performance indicators).

The Korean government support for ICRD includes (1) international cooperation growing out of individual public R&D projects (interpersonal); (2) projects sponsored by MOST (corporate and team collaboration); and (3) ICRDs by other ministries. The first component is expected to account for the largest and the most important international cooperation efforts, but little information is available for analysis. Currently, the Korean government is building a database for national R&D projects, but it is not yet possible to collect the information on ICRD activities systematically. An informal survey by KISTEP indicates that 7.2 percent of national R&D projects in 2000 involve some form of international cooperation. A follow-up survey estimates that this share was reduced to 4.3 percent in 2001. Only two agencies have dedicated ICRD budgets: MOST and MOCIE (Ministry of Commerce, Industry, and Energy). International cooperation represents a very small part of the budgets of other ministries. Therefore, only international cooperation sponsored by MOST and MOCIE is described in this report.

According to MOST, overseas R&D investment by Korean sources (public or private sector) totaled 605.7 billion won ($502 million) in 1998 and 495.5 billion won ($443 million) in 1999, shown in Table 2.4. The proportion of overseas investment to the total national R&D expenditures were 5.3 percent in 1998 and 4.2 percent in 1999. Most overseas R&D expenditures were made by private

Table 2.3

Korean Government Policies Supporting ICRD

International Science and Technology Agreements	International S&T agreements with 135 countries (effective for 130) S&T agreements with 43 countries implemented Atomic cooperation agreements with 14 countries implemented
S&T International Cooperative Infrastructure Building	Stationing S&T diplomats to 8 countries (including the U.S.) 14 ICRD cooperation centers in 6 countries (KIMM-MIT in the U.S.) 5 overseas branches of the Government Research Institutes (one in U.S.) 13 overseas local labs of Korean universities in 5 countries Overseas corporate R&D: 70 subsidiaries and 13 research centers
Human and Information Exchange	Exchange with the U.S., Germany, etc.; Post-doc training; and brain pool S&T information: KOSEN (Korean Scientists & Engineers Network) and OSTIN (Overseas S&T Information Network)
ICRD	Binational ICRD activities with 30 countries Multinational ICRD

SOURCE: Choi et al., 2001.

Table 2.4

Korean R&D Spending Abroad, by Type of Institution, All Sources, 1998–1999

Types of Research-Performing Institutes	1998		1998 (private source)	1999	
Foreign universities & colleges	5,212	(0.9%)	4,146	5,731	(1.2%)
Foreign nonprofit institutes	5,717	(0.9%)	2,631	4,736	(1.0%)
Foreign governments	95	(0.0%)	50	699	(0.1%)
International institutes	890	(0.1%)	54	347	(0.1%)
Companies Overseas					
Joint companies	9,683	(1.6%)	9,683	205	(0.0%)
Subsidiaries	88,809	(14.7%)	88,809	1,209	(0.3%)
Affiliated companies	—		—	121	(0.0%)
Joint research institutes	153,173	(25.3%)	152,074	106,275	(21.4%)
Foreign companies	329,502	(54.4%)	296,534	372,487	(75.2%)
Subtotal	581,167	(95.9%)	547,100	481,611	(97.2%)
Others	12,676	(2.1%)	12,626	3,786	(0.8%)
Total	605,757	(100%)	566,607	495,496	(100%)
Total in US$ million[a]	502		469	433	

SOURCE: MOST homepage, http://www.most.go.kr/research-e/4-1.htm; MOST, 2000b.
[a]Exchange rate was 1,209 won/$ in 1998 and 1,145 won/$ in 1999.

enterprises (93.5 percent in 1998). The vast majority was invested in corporate alliances and private-sector research: The private sector granted less than 2 percent of overseas funds to foreign universities, nonprofit institutes, or international institutes. MOST's R&D evaluation study (2001) claims that the Korean government should play a more active role in investing in overseas R&D, in part to redress the imbalance in investment in public research.

Programs designed to sponsor ICRD with the United States include the following:

- The Korea-U.S. Industrial Technology Cooperation Fund, a channel for collaboration in industrial technology
- The Korea-U.S. Special Cooperative Program, promoting the exchange of scientists and engineers and sponsoring joint research projects (spending around $100 million annually)
- The Korea-U.S. S&T Cooperation Forum, held annually since 1993 to expedite joint cooperation in fields of mutual interests
- The Korea-U.S. S&T cooperation center near Washington, D.C.

The Korean government has crafted policies to take part in multinational ICRD:

- OECD: Korea is a full member of the Committee for Science and Technology Policy.
- APEC (Asia Pacific Economic Cooperation): The Korean government participated in APEC's Economic and Technical Cooperation (ECOTECH) activities including cooperation on industrial S&T, marine resources, regional energy, and development of human resources. MOST is currently implementing four Korea-initiated projects, and KISTEP is developing the APEC Science and Technology Network (ASTN) project by exchanging scientists and training engineers.
- Participation in international megascience projects: Korea is a partner in Intelligent Manufacturing System (IMS) as a regular member; the government is participating in a subprogram of the Large Hadron Collider (LHC); individual researchers are participating in the World Climate Research Program (WCRP) and in the International Geosphere-Biosphere Program (IGBP).

Ministry of Science and Technology (MOST)

MOST is the most active supporter of ICRD among Korean government agencies. The Vision 2025 plan by MOST (2000) guides Korea to change the R&D system from the current "domestically determined type" to the "globally networked type" in parallel with S&T internationalization, and suggests recommendations as follows:

- Incorporate the overseas sector in the national S&T innovation system

- Create an attractive R&D environment for Korea to emerge as a center of excellence

- Simultaneously push liberalization and overseas participation

- Comply with international R&D norms and standards

- Establish an institute that specializes in international S&T collaboration.

MOST has been actively pursuing a policy that promotes international cooperative R&D activities since 1985 with two axes: (1) a program to establish systems and institutions supportive of international cooperative R&D activities (ICRD infrastructures building); and (2) international research funding programs. Table 2.5 summarizes MOST's investments. S&T internationalization policies by MOST include: (1) enhancing access to frontier technology through S&T internationalization; (2) developing projects such as an overseas cooperative research center building, promoting joint research, human and information exchange; and (3) actively participating in consortia and committees of international S&T norm and standard development.

Since 1985, MOST has funded 1,590 projects that have some international components with a cumulative sum of 91 billion won ($72 million), resulting in 289 domestic and overseas patents and 1,982 publications as of 2000. The majority of the funds spent on collaboration is dedicated to bilateral rather than multilateral cooperation. This is in contrast to the budgets of other scientifically advanced countries, where an emphasis is placed on multilateral cooperation. Cooperation with Japan, Russia, the United States, Germany, and France accounted for three-fourths of the total ICRD projects, according to MOST. The Korean-U.S. cooperative R&D projects accounted for 18 percent of the total ICRD projects during 1985–1997. When examined by subject, 25 percent of the Korean-U.S. cooperative R&D projects are related to new materials research, and 19 percent are related to mechatronics, two fields where Korea has strength.

KOSEF is a funding agency within MOST that supports international human and information exchange activities such as post-doctoral training of Korean scientists overseas, or foreign scientists in Korea. KISTEP manages the R&D program sponsored by MOST, and works as a specialized agency for S&T internationalization projects of MOST.

When implementing the ICRD projects, MOST decides the overall direction and priority, and then KISTEP announces the competition through the domestic media and selects from applied proposals. At this writing, only Korean researcher/institutes were eligible to become a principal investigator of a cooperative project, but MOST reports that it plans to change this into an open system, allowing the foreign researcher/institutes to apply directly as a principal investigator.

As a part of the S&T international cooperation infrastructure building efforts, MOST established the Korea Institute of Machinery and Materials–Massachusetts Institute of Technology (KIMM-MIT) center at MIT. This is a ten-year project that began in 1998 and is slated to continue through 2008. Currently, five R&D projects are in progress, with a total budget of about $1 million annually. An evaluation by the Korean National S&T Council urged MOST to sharpen the program's strategic focus and improve links with industry. These changes are expected for this program in the near future.

Ministry of Commerce, Industry and Energy (MOCIE)

MOCIE sponsors ICRD activities and supports international industrial technology cooperation projects. Most of its international cooperation is based on bilateral agreements, mainly with Israel, Australia, Brazil, the United States, Japan, and the European Union. MOCIE's international cooperation budget was 6.5 billion won ($5.2 million) in 2000. In sponsoring ICRD, the agency gives priority to what it terms "generic" technologies—those expected to become platforms for the development of many different kinds of technology-based products. If a principal investigator is part of a nonprofit organization such as a university, participation by the private sector is required.

The Institute for Industrial Technology Evaluation and Planning (ITEP) manages the R&D program sponsored by MOCIE. MOCIE supports the Korean-U.S. industrial technology cooperation and investment infrastructure, based on the MOU between Korea and the U.S. Committee for Business Cooperation established in 1995. MOCIE also supports building an international technology cooperation network, disseminating international technology information, and promoting frontier technology-oriented cooperation. These activities were supported with a budget of 3.6 billion won ($2.9 million) in 2001. Table 2.5 summarizes MOCIE's investments.

Other Policies and Programs

In an independent study, Yn and Yim (1999) analyzed Korean ICRD policies and found:

(1) The primary form of support systems for international R&D is the research bases established in foreign countries, and this seems to be rather satisfactory in view of the demand from Korea's research community.

(2) The government international R&D programs support hundreds of research projects annually, but most are small projects (less than $10,000 on average), initiated by individual university professors and rather clustered in the basic research area. The degree of cooperation with foreign researchers is diverse, ranging from nominal cooperation to a fully integrated activity, but nonetheless large-scale research projects led by Korean scientists have not yet appeared.

(3) The government aims to allocate the limited R&D resources with a focused strategy, but the focuses between the two policy axes appear to be misaligned. In other words, while the establishment of cooperative research centers and human exchange activities is focused on Russia, the ICRD activities are concentrated on the United States, Japan, and China.

Yn and Yim (1999) recommended that MOST strategically shift its overly diversified, piecemeal, and dependent research programs more toward large-scale programs initiated by Korean scientists in line with national research needs. They also emphasized the need to increase the budget for international programs as well as foster a better coordination between the two policy axes.

Since 1990, Korea has supported Centers of Excellence—including science research centers (SRCs), engineering research centers (ERCs), and regional research centers (RRCs). Once selected, the centers receive government funding for up to nine years provided that every three-year interim evaluation shows good progress. As of 2001, 36 SRCs, 47 ERCs, and 37 RRCs have been funded, and the total number of these centers is expected to increase to 150 by 2002.

KOSEF supports the SRCs and ERCs to establish overseas Korean labs at universities in developed countries. Yn and Yim (1999) interviewed personnel at three overseas Korean labs and reported the following:

(1) The purposes of the establishment of SRC/ERC overseas Korean labs are: (1) playing a similar role to that of the overseas branch of Korean research

Table 2.5

Korean Government Spending on S&T Internationalization in 1998 and 1999

Ministry	Category		Project	1998	1999
MOST	Cooperative infrastructure building	International S&T cooperative base development	ISTC (International S&T Center)	1,198	1,000
			Korea-Russia joint research center	1,185	1,000
			Korea-UK aviation joint research center	1,402	1,315
			Korea-China joint research center	775	1,000
			KIMM-MIT cooperation	495	1,000
			KIST-Europe center	958	800
		Subtotal		6,013 17%	6,115 20%
	Human and information exchange	International S&T cooperative base development	Asia-Pacific Theoretical Physics Center	788	432
			Korea-Russia human exchange	4,574	4,200
			Foreign S&T information database	0	400
			APEC S&T Network (ASTN) development	405	450
			S&T cooperation events	760	0
			Korean-US cooperation	520	400
		International S&T cooperation	Korean-UK cooperation	780	900
			International technology cooperation	1,478	1,200
		KOSEF	Training of Korean researchers overseas	6,665	3,154
			Overseas Korean scientists support	326	316

Table 2.5—continued

Ministry	Category	Project	1998		1999	
	International joint research	S&T Olympic support	437		518	
		Korea-Humbolt project	1,049		815	
		Invitation of foreign brains	2,716		1,925	
		Subtotal	20,498	58%	14,710	49%
		ICRD 162 International cooperative R&D projects	8,279		8,467	
		Atomic ICRD 17 Atomic ICRD projects	792		800	
		Subtotal	9,071	25%	9,267	31%
		Sum	35,582		30,092	
		Sum (in US$ thousands)	29,431		26,281	
MOCIE	Human and information exchange	International industrial technology cooperation projects	5,610		5,200	
		ASEAN technology transfer and training programs	274		226	
		Subtotal	5,884	60%	5,426	47%
	Joint research	Subtotal 51 ICRD projects	4,001	40%	5,999	53%
		Sum	9,885		11,425	
		Sum (in US$ thousands)	8,176		9,978	
Total		Cooperative infrastructure building	6,013	13%	6,115	15%
		Human and information exchange	26,382	58%	20,136	49%
		International joint research	13,072	29%	15,266	37%
		Sum	45,467		41,517	
		Sum (in US$ thousands)	37,607		36,259	

SOURCE: MOST, 2000a.

centers; (2) taking advantage of overseas S&T resources by direct investment at foreign universities; and (3) training Korean scientists in foreign universities, particularly absorbing tacit knowledge.

(2) The benefits for foreign universities in accepting the establishment of the SRC/ERC local labs are: (1) utilizing the Korean graduate students and post-doc researchers; (2) receiving small but significant research funds; (3) citing their experience in international cooperation when they apply for research funds from their own countries.

(3) The implications of supporting local labs are: (1) establishing access to the research network in developed countries; (2) promoting human exchange and training including post-doc and graduate student training and international workshops, and (3) facilitating international cooperative research. Yn and Yim point out that the establishment of local labs does not have to be preceded by joint research, but rather, it may be better that joint research activities naturally lead to the establishment of local labs.

(4) SRC/ERC overseas Korean labs can be classified into three groups: (1) joint research-oriented type, (2) advanced S&T absorption-oriented type, and (3) mutual human exchange-oriented type. However, the lack of research budget from the Korean government limits the effect of joint research.

In addition to SRC/ERC, Korea has tried to build world-class domestic institutes to attract foreign researchers. The Korea Institute for Advanced Studies (KIAS), established in 1996, has over 180 visiting scholars from home and abroad, and has organized numerous international conferences and workshops, in which several world-renowned scientists have participated. The Asia-Pacific Center for Theoretical Physics (APCTP) was placed in Korea in 1997. It was designed to provide young scientists with training opportunities within their reach and to facilitate contact with leading-edge information and development in basic science. Both KIAS and APCTP give Asia-Pacific scientists an opportunity to work together and advance the regional level of basic sciences.

The Role of Science and Technology Agreements

Korea and the United States have used formal and informal agreements to encourage S&T cooperation. Science and technology agreements, sometimes called International Science and Technology Agreements (ISTAs) range from legally binding treaties approved by legislatures to letters of correspondence between agencies with no legally binding authority.

The U.S. government has signed both an executive-level "umbrella" ISTA and dozens of agency-level ISTAs with Korea. The umbrella ISTA agreement was first signed in 1976, and amended in 1993 and 1999. It remains in effect today. The 1993 agreement prescribed the allocation of intellectual property rights (IPRs) resulting from mutual cooperation and established the Joint Committee on Science and Technology Cooperation that would conduct a joint review of cooperative activities on a biennial basis.

The DoS reports that, additionally, there are 22 active ISTAs between the United States and Korea signed at the agency level; however, this number likely understates the total number of active agency-level agreements. The subjects of the agreements range broadly in the targeted areas of S&T. Environmental and earth sciences, aeronautics, and agreements to cooperate in general and basic science claim the highest number of agreements. The agencies reporting the largest number of agreements with Korea are DoE, NASA, and the DoC.

S&T agreements can be an important indicator of national interest in S&T cooperation. However, ISTAs are non-funded, diplomatic-level agreements that have no associated budget authority. Many ISTAs are never fully implemented because of a lack of funds from one or both signatories. Sometimes, an agreement is made to cooperate and an ISTA is signed to establish the parameters of this cooperation. In other cases, S&T projects take place without reference to an ISTA. Relying on a list of ISTAs to provide a picture of the binational S&T relationship between the United States and Korea can be misleading when the goal is to identify the range and character of cooperation. Possibilities for using ISTAs to enhance the Korean-U.S. relationship are discussed in Section 4.

3. Views of Collaborating Scientists on the Korean-U.S. Relationship

The RAND research team spoke to 20 U.S.-based scientists and engineers who have worked with Korean researchers in the past several years. About half of the researchers were identified through the use of RaDiUS, a RAND database that tracks federal R&D. These researchers, in turn, introduced the RAND research team to the rest of the interlocutors. We found during the interviews that half of the respondents were originally from Korea, although they were not prechosen based on this fact. They came to the United States initially for their graduate training and have stayed on to develop their careers in the United States. Comments from these ten interviewees reflect considerable familiarity with Korean society and the Korean scientific establishment. They also had sharper criticisms than others about S&T policies and institutions in Korea.

In the majority of projects covered in these interviews, scientists and engineers in Korea and the United States chose to collaborate because of shared interests in certain research questions. Generally, these bottom-up, curiosity-driven R&D collaborations between researchers in Korea and the United States were bilateral, involving generally one researcher/organization in each country. In a few instances, U.S. researchers served as advisors to projects in Korea but did not participate in the actual research collaboration. These collaborations represent a broad range of scientific research areas, including mechanical engineering, molecular biology, materials, mathematics, computer science, plasma, aerospace, high-energy theory physics, and chemistry. Most projects discussed in these interviews met their research goals, although some were considered more successful collaborations than others by the researchers.

In two-thirds of the projects discussed in the telephone interviews, respondents said that collaborative relationships began with face-to-face meetings between the partners. These meetings occurred at an international conference or on a campus in the United States when the Korean researcher was a graduate student, visiting professor, or research fellow. (This corresponds with data on Korean student and scholarly exchanges in the United States.) In several cases, collaborations that began in the United States continued after the Korean researcher returned to work in Korea, and thus the project became an international R&D collaboration. Most respondents reported that they continue to exchange information and data with their Korean counterparts after completing a formal project. Both sides see such communication as beneficial to their respective research.

When face-to-face interaction occurred in a collaboration, the Korean side was more likely to visit the United States than vice versa. Visits are typically short, lasting one to two weeks. This tendency might be explained by the greater availability of travel funds for Korean researchers to visit the United States and their motivation to do so. One respondent remarked that, to his knowledge, Korean scientists typically obtain more support from KOSEF for research with U.S. and other foreign scientists than they do when working with domestic partners. This larger support perhaps takes into consideration travel expenses for the researcher. For U.S. researchers, in comparison, funding for international R&D collaboration is limited. Moreover, associated time and financial costs involved in communication, overseas visits, or dealing with grant and university bureaucracies can be so high that they discourage international collaboration.

The U.S. scientists we interviewed chose to work with researchers in Korea because they see scientific research value in such international collaboration. The vast majority of respondents indicated that although the research could have been done without collaboration with scientists in Korea, progress might have been slower and the results less rigorous. (Only in a few cases did interviewees say that the work could not have been done without collaboration with their Korean counterparts, e.g., two projects on enzyme reaction mechanisms and molecular biosynthesis of antibiotics.)

A motivation for international collaboration might be revealed in this common response from several of the U.S. scientists we interviewed: International collaborations are not so much an explicit decision as they are the natural outcome of scientists meeting each other, discovering shared research interests, and deciding to work together. International collaborations are also the natural outcome when U.S. scientists try to find the best (or most appropriate) person to work with on a research question. They look for expertise and knowledge, and pay little attention to citizenship or residence of their collaborators. In a few cases, the respondents indicated that they also choose to collaborate in order to learn about different perspectives or approaches to scientific problems.

When asked about communication and information exchange methods that were critical to the success of the project, the overwhelming response was that face-to-face interaction between collaborators is the key method. Several U.S. and Korean collaborators had known each other previously through student-teacher relationships or visiting fellowships and sabbaticals. Many were introduced to each other through third parties or met at professional meetings such as workshops and conferences. Respondents underlined the importance of establishing a sense of rapport with counterparts through face-to-face interaction to support later communication via the Internet, telephone, and other means. In most cases, Korean researchers come to the United States for short visits that last from one week to several months, and sometimes as long as a full year (post-doctoral fellowships or sabbaticals in the United States). For those involved in experimental science the ability to interact in real time, exchange views, test ideas, and work in laboratories adds much to advance scholarship and skills of the collaborators—particularly those on the Korean side—and contributes to the success of their research.

We asked interviewees to comment on the caliber of their Korean counterparts. Most indicated that they find their Korean counterparts highly capable and in some instances world class in the areas of research they are pursuing. One U.S. scientist indicated that his research partner in Korea is on the cutting edge of robotics research. He also reported that Korea is world class in many areas of mechanical engineering, and is stronger than the United States in some areas. Most of the collaborations covered in these interviews involved Korean researchers affiliated with the top universities in Korea. These Korean researchers are not only some of the best in the country (and the world), but their home institutions also have some of the best facilities by world standards and they receive considerable research funds from their universities or the Korean government. Hence, in a few cases where the U.S. side has facilities inferior to the Korean side, the U.S. researchers depended on the Korean researchers to conduct the experiments or computational work.

Graduate students are also frequently involved in these projects. Interviewees generally find Korean graduate students highly competent and hardworking. Sometimes their involvement in an international collaboration leads them to continue their studies or training in the United States, thus cultivating another generation of Korean researchers active in collaboration with U.S. scientists and engineers.

NSF and KOSEF provided funding support for most of the projects reviewed in the interviews involving international collaborations between researchers in Korea and the United States. Typically, NSF funds support travel and some research-related expenses for the U.S. side, while the Korean side is frequently supported by KOSEF. Other sources for Korean scientists identified in these interviews were KIMM and university departmental funds, while for U.S. researchers university department funds are a common source.

Interviewees were asked to comment on fields where stronger Korean-U.S. S&T ties might be useful in the next decade. Considering that these scientists are experts in their own fields, they chose to speak only on potentials for strengthening collaboration in their own areas of research. Most gave a positive response to furthering Korean-U.S. S&T collaboration overall and many have plans to continue both informal and formal collaboration with Korean scientists and engineers, but they were unable to point to any particular fields or areas of research as priorities between the two countries. Many feel that Korean scientists are becoming more proficient (e.g., better trained in the fundamentals) and the younger ones are particularly proactive and more confident about their work. As a result, many conclude that working with Korean scientists and engineers would help improve endogenous scientific capacity in Korea and help the Korean scientific community to contribute to world science.

However, some questioned what the U.S. side has to gain from intensifying S&T relations with Korea. A few pointed to this also as a reason for the lack of interest among U.S. graduate students in seeking research fellowships in Korea or fostering their own research ties with peers in Korea. Only one interviewee believed that collaborations with Korean scientists would help advance U.S. science. This particular scientist was concerned that fewer U.S. scientists are involved in enzyme research, which is critical to advancing U.S. research in proteomics. Thus, he considers collaboration with Korean scientists a way to remedy this domestic labor shortage in the United States.

U.S. researchers also serve as agents to deliver information to their research collaborators in Korea. U.S. scientists are frequently asked to deliver lectures to faculty or graduate student audiences on the latest research trends and breakthroughs in the United States. None of the respondents reported any negative sentiment toward this demand on their time in Korea. In fact, many explicitly indicated that such presentations in Korea help to facilitate interaction and support efforts to identify research problems for collaboration between U.S. and Korean scientists and among Korean researchers themselves.

Finally, one respondent stressed that Korean graduate students and post-doctoral fellows should acquire a sufficient level of English proficiency before coming to the United States to begin their visit. He had encountered a number of Korean graduate students and post-doctoral fellows who struggled with language and communication problems in their first or second year, thus compromising their training and research. He further urged Korean companies to provide funding support for Korean graduate students and post-doctoral fellows in the United States.

54

In a similar survey, Yn and Yim (1999) interviewed 55 Korean researchers involved in the MOST projects and 110 Korean researchers involved in KOSEF projects carried out in 1998. They found that the ages of participants in partnering countries are higher, implying, according to Yn and Yim, that many researchers of partner countries were the supervisors of Korean researchers during their doctoral studies. Half of sampled projects were basic research, one-fourth were applied research, and the rest were development research. From the self-evaluation on the level of the ICRD, Korean researchers believe that the ICRD activities performed by Koreans are more than just work at a subcontracting level, and most of them believe that Korean researchers conduct research as competently as foreign partners. However, they are not confident about the Korean capacity to lead the larger-scale ICRD projects. Korean researchers answered that their objectives are: (a) the goals set out by the team in the research proposal; (b) publication of research papers; (c) preliminary research for larger-scale research; (d) developing an international network; (e) patent development; (f) building the overseas research base; (g) training researchers/graduate students; (h) hosting collaborative workshops; and (i) accessing equipment in a megascale government project.

4. Opportunities for Enhancing the Korean-U.S. S&T Relationship

The S&T relationship between Korea and the United States is in the process of shifting away from what might have been called a "senior-junior" relationship or a "center-periphery" relationship toward a more balanced relationship between scientifically advanced countries. As S. C. Chung (2001) has noted, Korea's transition to world-class S&T capacity has tracked with the transition of the scientific community overall toward global R&D. This has resulted from a deliberate policy to move Korea from foreign assistance to reciprocal multinational cooperation. Happily, Korea's transition has coincided with, and been able to take advantage of, the global information revolution. Korea is one of the most highly networked societies in the world, allowing researchers to take full advantage of dynamic networks emerging in global science. These transitions present opportunities for policymakers in both countries to consider shifts in priorities and perhaps a reorganization of the binational relationship.

The binational relationship still retains a number of characteristics and features that were crafted under a center-periphery model while Korea was developing its S&T base. Some of the features of this relationship, such as the special cooperative program sponsored by NSF and MOST, are no longer optimal. In order to enhance the relationship, it may be beneficial to restructure it to better fit both the changing nature of global S&T and the changing dynamics between the two countries. Figure 4.1 illustrates this change: As many factors converge to encourage a greater networked dynamism in science, more and more projects emerge in the spontaneous-distributed quadrant. Hierarchically organized and structured research projects—while still valid for many subjects—are increasingly being displaced by dynamic, networked projects that rely on distributed, coordinated research activities.

This emerging organization of science—allowing researchers to work in their home laboratories and link with others around the world—has considerable benefits for the Korean-U.S. relationship. Although the two countries are so far apart geographically, they have a close relationship in science. Their relationship could become a model of using ICT to further enhance collaboration. Using ICT means that resources will be more effectively shared, that the cost of travel and relocation of scholars will be reduced, and that real-time tasks can be allocated

RAND *MR1644-4.1*

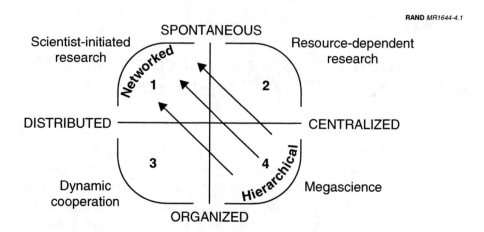

Figure 4.1—Organizational Structure of ICRD: Information Flows

and conducted in several places. This distributed allocation of science helps build capacity in a number of places, further enhancing the dynamism and benefits of the relationship.

Forging a More Balanced Relationship

It is widely recognized that the United States is currently the world center for science. It has been recently recognized that Korea has improved its scientific capacity to the point where it is among the scientifically advanced countries, at least in some important fields (Wagner et al., 2001). This fact leads to several discussion points for enhancing the Korean-U.S. relationship:

- Point: An initial premise might be that it is more to the advantage of Korea than to the United States to collaborate in science. In other words, the premise is that the United States has little to gain scientifically from the relationship. If we assume that the center-periphery model is valid here, and it is arguable that it is, then it would make sense for Korea (and for other countries) to collaborate, imitate, and adapt the scientific system practiced in the United States in order to build up its own capacity.

  Counterpoint: While the center-periphery model has many points for consideration, it does not account for the global dynamic networks that have emerged on top of the national science systems. This metanetwork creates "invisible colleges" of experts to which U.S. scientists seek (as well they should) to be a party. Accordingly, a vibrant collaborative relationship in the fields where Korea has significant strength is in the interests of the United

States as well as Korea. Moreover, Luukkonen et al. (1992) have shown that in a specific discipline, one country can become an intellectual center, with others seeking to collaborate with it. This phenomenon does not require a country to have the largest R&D investment, just a well thought-out strategy. Thus, Korea could take the lead in specific fields where it has strength or interest, and the United States could benefit from the enhanced investment.

- Point: The United States is among the world leaders in almost all fields of science, suggesting, again as an initial premise, that it would make sense for Korea to seek to collaborate with the United States in any field in which it seeks to build capacity.

  Counterpoint: Collaboration has been shown to be an effective method of capacity building (Wagner et al., 2001). However, an unequal collaborative relationship based on capacity building creates dependencies and feeds a perception of inferiority that may not be in the best interests of Korea over the long run. Collaborating in the areas of the *greatest strength* makes more sense, based on what we are learning about the dynamics of cooperation among scientifically advanced countries. It would be useful to match collaborations where Korea has strength—physics, chemistry, and an emerging capability in biomedical research—as a way to target areas for cooperation.

- Point: Moving the relationship to a new level may require new government-to-government agreements and new programs to target areas of strength.

  Counterpoint: Although a restructured ISTA agreement may be useful, and new programs may help shift targets, this may not be the best way to enhance the relationship. Successful collaborations work from the bottom up (they are identified by scientists themselves), are peer reviewed, and result from shared interests rather than common targets. The relationships among the scientifically advanced countries are robust because they encompass the interactions of hundreds of individual scientists seeking to work with the best people in their fields.

In summary, special emphasis in the bilateral relationship should be placed on collaborating in areas of strength and common interest, should take advantage of ICT and the infrastructural investments in both countries, and should be bottom-up and peer reviewed. Restructuring the Korean-U.S. relationship to better match the enhanced position of Korea and to reflect the networked, distributed nature of global science cannot be done in a single stroke. In the near term, enhancements may need to be tailored to the type of scientific activities that are of interest. Moreover, as we have discussed, the extent to which science policy has an effect on the nature of the S&T conducted between the two nations depends heavily on the funding source, the nature of the scientific questions, the location of resources, the interests of scientists, and so on. Policymakers have a direct influence over only a small portion of the overall relationship. Thus, an enhanced relationship would have aspects of each of these features, taking account of the dynamics of different types of sciences and the characteristics of collaboration as well as roles for the private sector. For other parts, setting an agenda or providing infrastructure can help, but only in an indirect way. In still other cases, policymakers have no impact on the nature of the relationship. The following section discusses enhancements as they may apply to each of the four quadrants of Figure 4.1, ones that broadly represent the dynamics of collaboration. Table 4.1 summarizes the points in each of the four sections.

Maximizing Spontaneous-Distributed Activities

Spontaneous-distributed ICRD activities, located in quadrant 1 of Figure 4.1, are those activities emerging from the interests of individual scientists and then taking place as physically remote interchanges from an investigator's home lab. If we were to refer back to the "iceberg" in Figure 1.7, these activities would be "below the waterline" in the team section. These types of projects are often funded through grants made either to the individual investigator or to a research institution. Each grant is generally small compared with the cost of participating in a megascience project. Links among researchers are often robust and active, and may include representatives from more than one scientific discipline. The learning that takes place as part of the research is often contained within the team during the course of the project, which, on average, may be a period of three years, but the end results are usually codified in a scientific journal paper.

International partners in these types of projects often come from similar institutions (e.g., university labs, metrology labs) within scientifically advanced countries. As we have found in other research, collaboration is most successful when the capacity of the participants to conduct research is roughly equivalent (Wagner et al., 2001). The projects are time-limited, and, in the majority of cases, the links between the researchers become "quiet" when the project has ended.

Table 4.1

Characteristics of Participation in Different Types of ICRD

	Corporate → Team → Interpersonal			
Functions and Organizational Issues	Organized-centralized ICRD: megascience	Organized-distributed ICRD: Human Genome Project	Spontaneous-Centralized ICRD: global climate change research"	Spontaneous-distributed ICRD: teams
Methods of funding	Institutional funding, often centralized in a single organization run by a supranational staff; national funds pooled	Contracts or grants generally provided to teams based on peer review; funds sometimes provided directly to institutions; national funds sometimes pooled	Mixed financing, sometimes directly to institutions, others in pools of funds to teams of international researchers	Grant-based research, usually to an individual or small team; ICRD participants are self-funded
Entry, interaction costs for government participation	High costs associated with joining and maintaining a position in large-scale equipment investments; interactions can require extended visits	Medium costs involved in joining an established project and supporting national researchers; interactions involve ICT, conferencing	Medium-to-high costs of conducting equipment-based experiments, sharing data; interactions can require expensive travel	Low cost overall, project-based research; interactions use ICT
Organizational structure	Hierarchical/structured, with researchers sharing common research goals, ongoing research, and findings through a centralized program or through a well-defined set of core journals	Networked/structured, researchers choose topics and conduct experiments remotely, share results with larger program	Hierarchical/structured, concepts about what research to pursue being suggested by groups of researchers; data shared with large groups	Networked/unstructured, with researchers creating networks that interact based on project needs
Government Influence	High → Medium → Low			

Table 4.1—continued

	Corporate → Team → Interpersonal			
Style of knowledge output	Codified, with researchers writing findings and sharing these with colleagues and a wider scientific community	Tacit-experiential, with researchers first learning from each other as the work proceeds, sharing know-how with a larger group; publication follows	Codified, data driven, with researchers pooling knowledge into a larger set of data that is drawn upon by many	Tacit-experiential, with researchers first learning from each other as the work proceeds; publication follows
National-level partnerships	"Top-down," heterogeneous partnerships involving advanced and developing countries, researchers from small and large institutions, funding sometimes provided from nongovernmental organizations	Mixed-homogeneous, with scientific goals guiding national investments; governments and industry often involved in organization, funding	Mixed-heterogeneous, with scientific goals set at the global level, governments and industry involved in agenda-setting, participants from advanced and developing countries, small and large institutions	"Bottom-up," homogeneous and unstable, researchers generally coming from similar institutions in scientifically advanced countries, partnerships forming and breaking up based on research question
Government Influence	High → Medium → Low			

Examples of these types of projects between Korean and U.S. researchers include:

- A joint study on agent-based cross-language information retrieval.[10]

- A comparative study of the prevention of dental problems in the United States and Korea.

- Joint studies on alternative energy sources.

---

[10]Researchers from Sookmyung Women's University in Seoul are working on this project with researchers at the Language Technologies Institute of Carnegie Mellon University. The Korean language offers many important and unique research challenges to digital libraries research. Solutions for information merging and retrieval from Korean/English corpora can be generalized to other non–alphabet based languages, including Japanese and Chinese.

One way to aid the growth of these relationships between Korean and U.S. scientists is to reduce transactions costs: sponsor workshops and symposia, offer liberal travel grants, and build bandwidth to ensure that work in progress as well as published material is widely available digitally to scientists in both countries. This could include creating virtual collaboration in specific fields of common interest, or holding a virtual conference on important research subjects.

Participating in Organized-Distributed Activities

Organized-distributed activities, quadrant 4 in Figure 4.1, are those where teams of participants from different countries share a common research goal. These are generally formal team partnerships such as the recently completed Human Genome Project and the ongoing IMS initiative. Like the spontaneous-distributed research activities, these types of distributed projects appear to be increasing in number and have attracted the interest of both policymakers and scientists. Often these projects will have mixed financing, with contributions from various sources and in varying modes (Wagner et al., 2002). These can include government and foundation grants, contracts, private-sector funding, and shared funding. The costs involved in initiating or joining programs like these can be significant. As a result, smaller countries are often unable to participate in them.

Communication within these team activities has features of both networks and hierarchies. Researchers communicate in ways similar to spontaneous-distributed research projects, but there is often a central coordinating office that also provides a communication function. At times, a central office may connect researchers to each other in order to facilitate connections. Data created in the course of these activities is often shared first within the research group and then published formally.

Organized-distributed research activities have the advantage of being able to include a range of partners, although often, the ability to provide financial contributions determines the cohort of participants. These programs can find ways to include private-sector partners, as well, and this can be a source of additional financing.

Lee (2001) suggests that Korea should reinforce its ongoing participation in these types of activities and join new projects such as the post–Human Genome Project and Human Frontiers Science Project. These types of activities offer significant benefits to Korea. Among the benefits are contacts with researchers from countries with which Korea has not been a traditional partner. This could help to extend Korea's international partnerships in a way that would enrich its science base.

Governments of both countries could consider several ways to enhance their relationship in the organized-distributed projects. Among these may be to consult with each other should either one consider proposing a new project to the international scientific community. A second way may be to set aside funds to encourage *teams* of Korean and U.S. researchers to participate in programs such as the IMS initiative. A third way may be to develop a joint evaluation tool with which to assess the effectiveness of existing activities and to offer this tool to other countries participating in team-based ICRD. A fourth way would be to invite private-sector ideas, financing, and leadership in dynamic research projects using this organizing principle.

Joining Organized-Centralized Activities

Organized-centralized activities, quadrant 3 in Figure 4.1, have traditionally been referred to as megascience projects. They include activities that are well known among the international scientific community such as CERN, ITER, and the ISS. These programs have characteristics of "corporate" collaboration, and are at the "tip of the iceberg" in Figure 1.7. Funding is often contributed by member governments to a shared pot, creating a single location and a supranational staff. They often involve the building of expensive research facilities such as a synchrotron.

Lee (2001) suggests that Korea initiate Korean-led megascience projects utilizing existing facilities like Pohang Collider Laboratory and Asia Pacific Theoretical Physics Center, and establish a megascience supporting system. Indeed, participating in these types of projects can bring prestige and excellent contacts along with them. Nevertheless, the costs involved are also high and require a multiyear commitment. As such, they tend to crowd out other types of R&D activities that may in fact help build a more robust international network.

The organization of these activities has traditionally been hierarchical, with researchers sharing common goals. While multidisciplinary studies are found within these programs, they generally focus on the research questions of concern to a single discipline of science, such as high-energy physics or aeronautics. The results of the research are usually codified in publications or in large-scale equipment. One benefit of this type of investment from the point of view of developing countries is that they use expensive facilities at marginal cost. However, researchers from countries that are not full members often find that their access to facilities is quite limited (OECD, 1997).

The growth of the Korean-U.S. relationship will probably benefit more from attention to growing the bottom-up research activities rather than focusing on this type of top-down investment. These are expensive activities with investments made in fields where the United States and Korea often have a strong relationship already—such as physics. It may be worth considering taking a balanced approach to all four types of ICRD: If such an approach were taken, attention to this megascience could wait while other types received more needed attention.

Choosing Among Spontaneous-Centralized Activities

Spontaneous-centralized activities, quadrant 2 in Figure 4.1, are those where a common research subject requires the collective efforts of interpersonal and team-based researchers. Common research questions include climate change, infectious disease, pollution, potable water supply, the science of the arctic, the health of the oceans, the movement of tectonic plates, and the welfare of endangered species. In many cases, the research activities surrounding these types of questions are globally coordinated—even if this is a loose configuration. Projects such as the Ocean Drilling Project and studies supporting the research questions before the Intergovernmental Panel on Climate Change have features of both spontaneous research and centralized organization. Funding for these projects is often mixed and can come from governments, nongovernmental organizations, and industry. The global nature of these questions means that international teams form with relative ease; an international team often enhances chances of receiving funding.

At times, participating in these projects can be expensive: Funding of the retrofitting of a ship to take part in arctic research or funding the launch of an atmosphere-monitoring satellite is costly. These types of investments mean that some coordinating function and government-to-government negotiation takes place. In addition, these projects can be data-intensive: Storing and making data accessible can also require a significant financial investment.

The global nature of the questions and the particularity of the location of the subjects of study mean that most governments have an interest in promoting this type of research. Organizations with global interests are also likely to fund these types of programs. The shared nature of the funding can often mean that some countries or individual research teams can participate without a great deal of up-front costs. An example of Korean-U.S. cooperation of this type is the analysis of the seismic response of the Jualien Containment Model, using extensive seismic response data recorded within the Jualien, Taiwan, 1/4-scale model of a nuclear containment structure to validate a set of mathematical models and computer codes. These mathematical models and computer codes have been used to calculate the seismic response of important structures when the effects of the interaction between the structure and the surrounding soil are significant. The Jualien experiment is being conducted by a consortium of organizations including the Electric Power Research Institute and the NRC in the United States, and institutions from Taiwan, Japan, Korea, and France.

Both governments have an interest in promoting this type of research on key global questions. These programs are perhaps the easiest to justify to stakeholders and legislatures. As a result, the Korean-U.S. relationship in these types of programs should be examined and possibly strengthened. One way to do this is to encourage the creation of data that can add to global understanding. A joint project to enhance efforts to create and share needed data on climate change, for example, would be a good way to enhance the binational relationship in a global context.

Conclusions and Policy Recommendations

Over the past two decades, in part due to explicit policy and in part to bottom-up growth, the United States has been the principal partner in Korea's quest to increase national S&T capacity. The United States has been Korea's most frequent partner in ICRD projects. U.S. universities have trained tens of thousands of Korean scientists and engineers. The United States government has maintained a special program to encourage the relationship, and has an active bilateral agreement to encourage cooperation. The United States has also been a key source for technology transfer, through investments by U.S. firms or imports of U.S. technology.

One outcome is strong collaborative research ties between scientists and engineers in the two countries. Another is enhanced S&T capacity in Korea as well as the rise of centers of excellence in specific fields. As the binational relationship has grown, and Korea has continued investments in the infrastructure needed to support a strong S&T sector, Korean science has emerged into world-class status in many fields. The development goals of both parties have borne fruit.

All this has helped Korea to transform from what Alice Amsden (1989) calls a "rapid imitator" to a country with a robust national innovation system. Indicators such as the number of patents awarded, publications in scientific journals, numbers of S&E professionals, and investment levels show that the country is rapidly joining the ranks of scientifically advanced nations. S&T policy reforms and new R&D initiatives are being implemented to firmly secure Korea's place in the community of scientifically advanced nations.

The position of the U.S. S&T community in world science has also changed. While the United States is at the frontier of most areas of scientific research, it is not the leader in every field. The nature of certain scientific problems and the costs of research for global problems provide an incentive for the United States to work cooperatively with other nations. The need for the United States to seek international partnerships, and to tap foreign centers of excellence, has also grown. The U.S. S&T sector has become increasingly interlinked with other nations, but it still remains (in terms of percentages of coauthorships, for example) less internationalized than other countries.

The United States continues to support S&T collaboration with Korea; support for the relationship in some science policy circles is strong. However, in other policy circles, concern grows as Korea continues to strengthen its competitive position in technology-based exports. The extent to which technology transfer from the United States is feeding Korean competitiveness remains a point for discussion. Some say that Korea benefits more from the bilateral S&T relationship than the United States does. Whether this is true is not the point: This uneven relationship may come into question as Korea's economic competitiveness continues to grow.

These factors suggest that the time has come for a new S&T policy agenda for the bilateral relationship. The information we provided above about the structure of collaboration, the strengths of the two countries, and the ways in which they form policy about international collaboration can certainly help to instruct a discussion about the relationship. In addition, the following points may also aid discussion.

1. Continue the shift away from a center-periphery relationship toward a "centers of excellence" model.

A shift away from a center-periphery relationship has already begun—for example, the AID no longer provides special science programs for Korea. Other special U.S. programs that target aid to Korean science should be phased out over time. Optimal cooperation will most likely result from bottom-up initiatives by individual scientists in both countries. Policies to encourage this, such as special Web-based links, data, and information, should be considered. A joint project on machine translation might help to improve a key technology that would aid the relationship.

Although we suggest that the U.S. government discontinue special funds for the bilateral relationship, special funds created by the Korean government to encourage U.S. researchers to work with Korean collaborators may continue to be useful. Many Korean researchers involved in international collaborations are from the top universities in Korea where research facilities are excellent. Opportunities to access these facilities physically or virtually may be welcomed by U.S. researchers. With the recovery of the Korean economy, private industry might be encouraged to enter into public-private partnerships and invest in these special research funds to encourage U.S. researchers to visit Korea.

2. Expand the dialogue on S&T infrastructure.

Bilateral cooperation on the costs of scientific infrastructure, with a point of identifying opportunities to leverage investments, would be useful. Such discussion can also address important issues related to scientific research, including policies and regulations on technology transfer, intellectual property rights protection, ethics in research, and environmental impact. This may be especially important in emerging scientific areas such as biotechnology, where laws and ethics are still in their early stages of development. Korea could sponsor international forums for discussion, support joint research to examine issues of concern to Korea (as well as both countries), and fund visits by U.S. experts to Korea to give lectures and sit on advisory panels. Such interaction may also help to better inform foreign experts and policymakers of efforts and conditions in Korea and facilitate dialogues to address potential problems and conflicts that might arise at the international level.

3. Further internationalize science in Korea.

Korea has been seeking to make its R&D environment more supportive of international R&D collaborations, and this appears to be a positive trend. The United States could benefit from reviewing Korea's set of policies in this regard. In addition, Korea can draw further lessons from the United States on the management of research laboratories to better support international R&D collaborations. Korea could use advisory boards that include scientists and engineers from the United States and other scientifically advanced countries to ascertain whether new measures, including review and evaluation of grant proposals, are implemented and how successful they are. The results would also be of use to the United States.

4. Diversify Korea's participation in global science.

Building on existing strong ties between researchers in both countries, Korea might consider increasing support for Korean researchers to be involved in multilateral R&D efforts based in the United States or led by the United States. However, Korea should move beyond its reliance on the bilateral relationship with the United States and seek to strengthen ties with other scientifically advanced countries. This might include steps toward increasing Korean involvement in distributed and large-scale international science projects and efforts to expand Korea's S&T ties with other countries. Apart from funding to support participation of Korean scientists in these efforts, Korea will also have to invest in sharing the cost of facilities, equipment, operations, maintenance, and administration of these multilateral R&D efforts wherever they might take place. Experience gained might help Korea to internationalize science in Korea and exercise S&T leadership at a regional and world level as articulated in its Vision 2025 plan.

Appendix A. The Index of Science and Technology Capacity

Index of Science and Technology Capacity

Country	(A) GNP per Capita	(B) Scientists and Engineers per Million Population	(C) S & T journal articles	(D) Expenditures for R & D (% of GNP)	(E) Institutions and Universities per Million Population	(F) Patents (USPTO and EPO)	(G) Adjusted Metric for Students Studying in USA
* United States	29240	3676	173233	2.6	63.65	315766	
* Japan	32350	4909	43655	2.8	1.74	117696	42198
* Germany	26570	2831	35294	2.4	6.59	61919	30475
* Canada	19170	2719	20989	1.7	91.75	12559	*25000*
Taiwan	*14634*	**7710**	4781	1.8	2.49	11289	15439
* Sweden	25580	3826	8227	3.8	9.78	7798	7415
* United Kingdom	21410	2448	39670	2.0	6.90	22081	25479
* France	24210	2659	26455	2.3	7.28	25730	14594
* Switzerland	39980	3006	6734	2.6	15.92	9076	7515
Israel	16180	*3977*	5227	2.4	30.17	3234	3589
* Korea, Rep	8600	2193	3960	2.8	0.97	9932	39470
* Finland	24280	2799	3786	2.8	30.58	3957	2318
* Australia	20640	3357	11830	1.8	24.79	4343	5332
* Iceland	*29946*	5339	*209*	1.5	4.34	39	388
* Denmark	33040	3259	3963	2.0	21.89	3001	2808
* Norway	34310	3664	2531	1.6	16.36	1321	3063
* Netherlands	24780	2219	10914	2.1	10.57	7877	4549
* Italy	20090	1318	16256	2.2	4.51	12021	6864
Russian Federation	2260	3587	17589	0.9	1.74	1103	12531
* Belgium	25380	2272	4711	1.6	12.35	4225	1803
* Ireland	18710	2319	1096	1.6	9.46	530	8732
* Austria	26830	1627	3269	1.5	22.47	3280	2628
Singapore	30170	2318	1082	1.1	5.31	523	1380
Slovenia	9780	2251	440	1.5	13.50	40	432
* New Zealand	14600	1663	2260	1.0	20.00	788	1921
* Spain	14100	1305	10557	0.9	3.07	1904	9040
* Luxembourg	*43475*	**1305**	*47*	**0.9**	1.11	209	95
Slovak Republic	3700	1866	1026	1.1	11.11	11	1912
Ukraine	980	2171	2428	*1.0*	0.58	105	3294
Belarus	2180	2248	589	1.1	1.18	15	775
* Czech Republic	5150	1222	1976	1.2	8.54	173	2717
Croatia	4620	1916	526	1.0	4.00	40	1171
Estonia	3360	2017	219	0.6	12.86	1	399
* Poland	3910	1358	4127	0.8	5.76	120	4081
Lithuania	2540	2028	181	0.7	2.43	7	877
Bulgaria	1220	1747	889	0.6	9.64	36	2326
Azerbaijan	480	2791		0.2	1.27	1	225
Cuba	*2194*	1612	147	0.8	2.16	12	80
China	750	454	7763	0.7	0.30	466	16175
Brazil	4630	168	3511	0.8	0.65	440	18127
* Hungary	4510	1099	1688	0.7	10.99	363	2312
* Portugal	10670	1182	968	0.6	4.20	77	893
Romania	1360	1387	721	0.7	2.67	240	1416
South Africa	3310	1031	2038	0.7	4.20	697	2999
India	440	149	8668	0.7	0.24	327	13064
* Greece	11740	773	2014	0.5	7.43	148	1842
Uzbekistan	950	1763	296	*0.3*	0.00	2	572
Latvia	2420	1049	148	0.4	9.17	4	474
Argentina	8030	660	1944	0.4	2.22	176	4255
Chile	4990	445	808	0.7	2.91	40	1530
* Mexico	3840	214	1758	0.3	0.56	272	12918
Moldova	380	330		0.9	0.93	3	451
Pakistan	470	72	254	0.9	0.43	2	2718
* Turkey	3160	291	1879	0.5	0.66	19	6160
Armenia	460	1485	166	*0.0*	1.05	1	330
Colombia	2470	0	178	*0.6*	0.56	20	5140
Macedonia	1290	1335		-	2.00	0	664
Venezuela	3530	209	398	0.5	1.34	109	3741
Mauritius	3730	361		0.4	7.50	1	85

Country	(H) GNP per Capita	(H) Scientists and Engineers per Million Population	(H) S & T journal articles	(H) Expenditures for R & D (% of GNP)	(H) Institutions and Universities per Million Population	(H) Patent (USPTO and EPO)	(H) Adjusted Metric for Students Studying in USA
* United States	2.42	2.20	13.15	2.72	5.72	11.13	
* Japan	2.75	3.15	3.15	2.94	-0.25	4.05	5.89
* Germany	2.15	1.55	2.50	2.43	0.22	2.06	4.13
* Canada	1.37	1.46	1.40	1.46	8.43	0.29	3.30
Taiwan	0.90	5.32	0.15	1.64	-0.18	0.25	1.86
* Sweden	2.04	2.32	0.41	4.19	0.52	0.12	0.65
* United Kingdom	1.61	1.25	2.84	1.84	0.25	0.64	3.38
* France	1.90	1.41	1.82	2.23	0.28	0.77	1.73
* Switzerland	3.55	1.68	0.30	2.68	1.12	0.17	0.67
Israel	1.06	2.43	0.18	2.36	2.49	-0.04	0.08
* Korea, Rep	0.27	1.05	0.08	2.97	-0.33	0.20	5.48
* Finland	1.91	1.52	0.07	2.91	2.53	-0.01	-0.12
* Australia	1.53	1.95	0.69	1.64	1.97	0.00	0.34
* Iceland	2.50	3.49	-0.21	1.27	0.00	-0.15	-0.41
* Denmark	2.82	1.88	0.08	1.84	1.69	-0.05	-0.04
* Norway	2.95	2.19	-0.03	1.36	1.16	-0.11	0.00
* Netherlands	1.96	1.07	0.62	2.01	0.60	0.13	0.22
* Italy	1.47	0.38	1.03	2.17	0.02	0.28	0.57
Russian Federation	-0.39	2.13	1.13	0.45	-0.25	-0.11	1.42
* Belgium	2.02	1.11	0.14	1.38	0.77	0.00	-0.19
* Ireland	1.32	1.15	-0.14	1.40	0.49	-0.14	0.85
* Austria	2.17	0.62	0.03	1.29	1.75	-0.04	-0.07
Singapore	2.52	1.15	-0.14	0.77	0.09	-0.14	-0.26
Slovenia	0.39	1.10	-0.19	1.20	0.88	-0.15	-0.40
* New Zealand	0.90	0.64	-0.05	0.66	1.51	-0.13	-0.17
* Spain	0.84	0.37	0.59	0.47	-0.12	-0.09	0.90
* Luxembourg	3.91	0.37	-0.22	0.47	-0.31	-0.15	-0.45
Slovak Republic	-0.24	0.80	-0.14	0.67	0.65	-0.15	-0.18
Ukraine	-0.53	1.04	-0.04	0.60	-0.36	-0.15	0.03
Belarus	-0.40	1.10	-0.18	0.69	-0.31	-0.15	-0.35
* Czech Republic	-0.09	0.30	-0.07	0.86	0.40	-0.15	-0.06
Croatia	-0.15	0.84	-0.18	0.64	-0.03	-0.15	-0.29
Estonia	-0.28	0.92	-0.21	0.04	0.82	-0.15	-0.40
* Poland	-0.22	0.41	0.10	0.30	0.14	-0.15	0.15
Lithuania	-0.36	0.93	-0.21	0.21	-0.18	-0.15	-0.33
Bulgaria	-0.50	0.71	-0.15	0.04	0.51	-0.15	-0.11
Azerbaijan	-0.58	1.52	-0.22	-0.42	-0.30	-0.15	-0.43
Cuba	-0.40	0.60	-0.21	0.40	-0.21	-0.15	-0.45
China	-0.55	-0.29	0.38	0.16	-0.39	-0.14	1.97
Brazil	-0.15	-0.51	0.05	0.36	-0.36	-0.14	2.27
* Hungary	-0.16	0.21	-0.09	0.19	0.64	-0.14	-0.12
* Portugal	0.48	0.27	-0.15	0.11	-0.01	-0.15	-0.33
Romania	-0.49	0.43	-0.17	0.24	-0.16	-0.15	-0.25
South Africa	-0.28	0.15	-0.07	0.21	-0.01	-0.13	-0.01
India	-0.58	-0.53	0.45	0.25	-0.40	-0.14	1.50
* Greece	0.60	-0.05	-0.07	-0.08	0.30	-0.15	-0.19
Uzbekistan	-0.53	0.72	-0.20	-0.31	-0.42	-0.15	-0.38
Latvia	-0.38	0.17	-0.21	-0.14	0.46	-0.15	-0.39
Argentina	0.21	-0.13	-0.07	-0.20	-0.21	-0.15	0.18
Chile	-0.11	-0.30	-0.16	0.19	-0.14	-0.15	-0.23
* Mexico	-0.23	-0.48	-0.09	-0.27	-0.36	-0.14	1.48
Moldova	-0.59	-0.39	-0.22	0.47	-0.33	-0.15	-0.40
Pakistan	-0.58	-0.59	-0.20	0.50	-0.38	-0.15	-0.05
* Turkey	-0.30	-0.42	-0.08	-0.11	-0.36	-0.15	0.46
Armenia	-0.58	0.51	-0.21	-0.64	-0.32	-0.15	-0.41
Colombia	-0.37	-0.64	-0.21	0.11	-0.36	-0.15	0.31
Macedonia	-0.49	0.39	-0.22	-0.70	-0.23	-0.15	-0.36
Venezuela	-0.26	-0.48	-0.19	-0.06	-0.29	-0.15	0.10
Mauritius	-0.24	-0.36	-0.22	-0.18	0.30	-0.15	-0.45

	(I)	(I)	(I)	(I)	(I)	(I)	(I)	(J)	
Weighting Factors:	1	3	2	3	1	1	1		
Country	GNP per Capita	Scientists and Engineers per Million Population	S & T journal articles	Expenditures for R & D (% of GNP)	Institutions and Universities per Million Population	Patent (USPTO and EPO)	Adjusted Metric for Students Studying in USA	INDEX	
* United States	0.20	0.55	2.19	0.68	0.48	0.93		**5.03**	Scientifically Advanced Nations
* Japan	0.23	0.79	0.52	0.74	-0.02	0.34	0.49	**3.08**	
* Germany	0.18	0.39	0.42	0.61	0.02	0.17	0.34	**2.12**	
* Canada	0.11	0.36	0.23	0.37	0.70	0.02	0.28	**2.08**	
Taiwan	0.07	1.33	0.02	0.41	-0.01	0.02	0.16	**2.00**	
* Sweden	0.17	0.58	0.07	1.05	0.04	0.01	0.05	**1.97**	
* United Kingdom	0.13	0.31	0.47	0.46	0.02	0.05	0.28	**1.73**	
* France	0.16	0.35	0.30	0.56	0.02	0.06	0.14	**1.60**	
* Switzerland	0.30	0.42	0.05	0.67	0.09	0.01	0.06	**1.60**	
Israel	0.09	0.61	0.03	0.59	0.21	0.00	0.01	**1.53**	
* Korea, Rep	0.02	0.26	0.01	0.74	-0.03	0.02	0.46	**1.49**	
* Finland	0.16	0.38	0.01	0.73	0.21	0.00	-0.01	**1.48**	
* Australia	0.13	0.49	0.12	0.41	0.16	0.00	0.03	**1.33**	
* Iceland	0.21	0.87	-0.03	0.32	0.00	-0.01	-0.03	**1.32**	
* Denmark	0.24	0.47	0.01	0.46	0.14	0.00	0.00	**1.31**	
* Norway	0.25	0.55	0.00	0.34	0.10	-0.01	0.00	**1.22**	
* Netherlands	0.16	0.27	0.10	0.50	0.05	0.01	0.02	**1.12**	
* Italy	0.12	0.09	0.17	0.54	0.00	0.02	0.05	**1.00**	
Russian Federation	-0.03	0.53	0.19	0.11	-0.02	-0.01	0.12	**0.89**	
* Belgium	0.17	0.28	0.02	0.35	0.06	0.00	-0.02	**0.86**	
* Ireland	0.11	0.29	-0.02	0.35	0.04	-0.01	0.07	**0.82**	
* Austria	0.18	0.15	0.00	0.32	0.15	0.00	-0.01	**0.80**	
Singapore	0.21	0.29	-0.02	0.19	0.01	-0.01	-0.02	**0.64**	Scientifically Proficient Nations
Slovenia	0.03	0.27	-0.03	0.30	0.07	-0.01	-0.03	**0.60**	
* New Zealand	0.07	0.16	-0.01	0.16	0.13	-0.01	-0.01	**0.49**	
* Spain	0.07	0.09	0.10	0.12	-0.01	-0.01	0.07	**0.44**	
* Luxembourg	0.33	0.09	-0.04	0.12	-0.03	-0.01	-0.04	**0.42**	
Slovak Republic	-0.02	0.20	-0.02	0.17	0.05	-0.01	-0.01	**0.35**	
Ukraine	-0.04	0.26	-0.01	0.15	-0.03	-0.01	0.00	**0.32**	
Belarus	-0.03	0.27	-0.03	0.17	-0.03	-0.01	-0.03	**0.32**	
* Czech Republic	-0.01	0.08	-0.01	0.22	0.03	-0.01	0.00	**0.29**	
Croatia	-0.01	0.21	-0.03	0.16	0.00	-0.01	-0.02	**0.29**	
Estonia	-0.02	0.23	-0.03	0.01	0.07	-0.01	-0.03	**0.20**	
* Poland	-0.02	0.10	0.02	0.08	0.01	-0.01	0.01	**0.19**	
Lithuania	-0.03	0.23	-0.03	0.05	-0.02	-0.01	-0.03	**0.16**	
Bulgaria	-0.04	0.18	-0.03	0.01	0.04	-0.01	-0.01	**0.14**	
Azerbaijan	-0.05	0.38	-0.04	-0.11	-0.02	-0.01	-0.04	**0.11**	
Cuba	-0.03	0.15	-0.04	0.10	-0.02	-0.01	-0.04	**0.11**	
China	-0.05	-0.07	0.06	0.04	-0.03	-0.01	0.16	**0.10**	
Brazil	-0.01	-0.13	0.01	0.09	-0.03	-0.01	0.19	**0.10**	
* Hungary	-0.01	0.05	-0.02	0.05	0.05	-0.01	-0.01	**0.10**	
* Portugal	0.04	0.07	-0.02	0.03	0.00	-0.01	-0.03	**0.07**	
Romania	-0.04	0.11	-0.03	0.06	-0.01	-0.01	-0.02	**0.05**	
South Africa	-0.02	0.04	-0.01	0.05	0.00	-0.01	0.00	**0.04**	
India	-0.05	-0.13	0.07	0.06	-0.03	-0.01	0.13	**0.04**	
* Greece	0.05	-0.01	-0.01	-0.02	0.02	-0.01	-0.02	**0.00**	
Uzbekistan	-0.04	0.18	-0.03	-0.08	-0.03	-0.01	-0.03	**-0.05**	Scientifically Developing Nations
Latvia	-0.03	0.04	-0.04	-0.03	0.04	-0.01	-0.03	**-0.07**	
Argentina	0.02	-0.03	-0.01	-0.05	-0.02	-0.01	0.01	**-0.09**	
Chile	-0.01	-0.07	-0.03	0.05	-0.01	-0.01	-0.02	**-0.11**	
* Mexico	-0.02	-0.12	-0.01	-0.07	-0.03	-0.01	0.12	**-0.14**	
Moldova	-0.05	-0.10	-0.04	0.12	-0.03	-0.01	-0.03	**-0.14**	
Pakistan	-0.05	-0.15	-0.03	0.12	-0.03	-0.01	0.00	**-0.15**	
* Turkey	-0.02	-0.10	-0.01	-0.03	-0.03	-0.01	0.04	**-0.17**	
Armenia	-0.05	0.13	-0.03	-0.16	-0.03	-0.01	-0.03	**-0.19**	
Colombia	-0.03	-0.16	-0.03	0.03	-0.03	-0.01	0.03	**-0.22**	
Macedonia	-0.04	0.10	-0.04	-0.17	-0.02	-0.01	-0.03	**-0.22**	
Venezuela	-0.02	-0.12	-0.03	-0.01	-0.02	-0.01	0.01	**-0.22**	
Mauritius	-0.02	-0.09	-0.04	-0.04	0.03	-0.01	-0.04	**-0.22**	

Figure A.1—Index of Science and Technology Capacity

Scientifically Developing Nations	Scientifically Lagging Nations

Iran
Benin
Yugoslavia, FR
Kuwait
Hong Kong, China
Costa Rica
Bolivia
Egypt, Arab Rep.
Mongolia
Turkmenistan
Indonesia
Malaysia
Uganda
Thailand
Kyrgyz Republic
United Arab Emirates
Togo
Tajikistan
Jordan
Tunisia
Philippines
Uruguay
Kazakhstan
Gabon
Saudi Arabia
Sri Lanka
Nepal
Burundi
Guatemala
Congo, Dem. Rep.
Iraq
Peru
Syrian Arab Republic
Central African Republic
Vietnam
Ecuador
Panama
Georgia
Burkina Faso
Guinea
Madagascar
Guinea-Bissau
Oman
Botswana
Jamaica
Lebanon
Nigeria
Libya
Trinidad Tobago
Kenya
Nicaragua
Bangladesh
Zimbabwe
Namibia
Senegal
Dominican Republic
El Salvador
Rwanda
Morocco
Papua New Guinea
Paraguay
Ghana
Zambia
Malawi
Honduras
Algeria
Tanzania
West Bank and Gaza
Côte d'Ivoire
Cameroon
Bosnia and Herzegovina
Lesotho
Albania
Gambia

Figure A.1—continued

	Scientifically Lagging Nations	(A)	(B)	(C)	(D)	(E)	(F)	(G)	(H)	(H)	(H)	(H)	(H)	(H)	(H)	(I)	(I)	(I)	(I)	(I)	(I)	(I)	(J)
Haiti		410	0		-	0.26	2	363	-0.59	-0.64	-0.22	-0.70	-0.39	-0.15	-0.41	-0.05	-0.16	-0.04	-0.17	-0.03	-0.01	-0.03	-0.50
Congo, Rep.		110	0		-	0.71	1	197	-0.62	-0.64	-0.22	-0.70	-0.35	-0.15	-0.43	-0.05	-0.16	-0.04	-0.17	-0.03	-0.01	-0.04	-0.50
Ethiopia		100	0		-	0.33	0	401	-0.62	-0.64	-0.22	-0.70	-0.39	-0.15	-0.40	-0.05	-0.16	-0.04	-0.17	-0.03	-0.01	-0.03	-0.50
Mali		250	0		-	0.57	0	143	-0.60	-0.64	-0.22	-0.70	-0.36	-0.15	-0.44	-0.05	-0.16	-0.04	-0.17	-0.03	-0.01	-0.04	-0.50
Mauritania		410	0		-	0.40	0	58	-0.59	-0.64	-0.22	-0.70	-0.38	-0.15	-0.46	-0.05	-0.16	-0.04	-0.17	-0.03	-0.01	-0.04	-0.50
Angola		380	0		-	0.06	0	231	-0.59	-0.64	-0.22	-0.70	-0.41	-0.15	-0.43	-0.05	-0.16	-0.04	-0.17	-0.03	-0.01	-0.04	-0.50
Sudan		290	0		-	0.14	0	219	-0.60	-0.64	-0.22	-0.70	-0.41	-0.15	-0.43	-0.05	-0.16	-0.04	-0.17	-0.03	-0.01	-0.04	-0.50
Yemen		280	0		-	0.00	0	306	-0.60	-0.64	-0.22	-0.70	-0.42	-0.15	-0.42	-0.05	-0.16	-0.04	-0.17	-0.03	-0.01	-0.03	-0.50
Sierra Leon		140	0		-	0.41	0	76	-0.61	-0.64	-0.22	-0.70	-0.38	-0.15	-0.45	-0.05	-0.16	-0.04	-0.17	-0.03	-0.01	-0.04	-0.50
Niger		200	0		-	0.30	0	46	-0.60	-0.64	-0.22	-0.70	-0.39	-0.15	-0.46	-0.05	-0.16	-0.04	-0.17	-0.03	-0.01	-0.04	-0.51
Cambodia		260	0		-	0.09	0	130	-0.61	-0.64	-0.22	-0.70	-0.41	-0.15	-0.44	-0.05	-0.16	-0.04	-0.17	-0.03	-0.01	-0.04	-0.51
Myanmar		282	0		-	0.02	1	150	-0.60	-0.64	-0.22	-0.70	-0.42	-0.15	-0.44	-0.05	-0.16	-0.04	-0.17	-0.03	-0.01	-0.04	-0.51
Mozambique		210	0		-	0.18	0	99	-0.61	-0.64	-0.22	-0.70	-0.40	-0.15	-0.45	-0.05	-0.16	-0.04	-0.17	-0.03	-0.01	-0.04	-0.51
Korea, Dem. Rep.		430	0		-	0.00	0	32	-0.58	-0.64	-0.22	-0.70	-0.42	-0.16	-0.46	-0.05	-0.16	-0.04	-0.17	-0.03	-0.01	-0.04	-0.51
Lao PDR		320	0		-	0.00	0	75	-0.60	-0.64	-0.22	-0.70	-0.42	-0.16	-0.45	-0.05	-0.16	-0.04	-0.17	-0.03	-0.01	-0.04	-0.51
Chad		230	0		-	0.00	0	46	-0.61	-0.64	-0.22	-0.70	-0.42	-0.16	-0.46	-0.05	-0.16	-0.04	-0.17	-0.03	-0.01	-0.04	-0.51
Eritrea		200	0		-	0.00	0	44	-0.61	-0.64	-0.22	-0.70	-0.42	-0.15	-0.46	-0.05	-0.16	-0.04	-0.17	-0.03	-0.01	-0.04	-0.51

(A) Gross national product per capita for 1998 [World Bank, World Development Indicators, 2000. http://www.worldbank.org/data/wdi2000/pdfs/tab1_1.pdf] Data from other sources, including United Nations Statistics [http://www.un.org/Depts/unsd/social/inc-eco.html], are indicated in italics.

(B) Number of scientists and engineers in R&D per 1 million population [World Bank, World Development Indicators 2000. http://www.worldbank.org/data/wdi2000/pdfs/tab5_12.pdf] Additional data obtained from the "Second European Report on Science and Technology Indicators" S-59, December 1997, EUR 17639 and the 1998 World Science Report, UNESCO, Paris., in all cases the most recent data accessible was used. Values from these additional sources are indicated in italics.

(C) Number of science and technology journal articles published in 1995-1997 average values [Science Indicators 2000, National Science Foundation]. Additional values (indicated in italics) were obtained from "Second European Report on Science and Technology Indicators" S-59, December 1997, EUR 17639 and are measures for 1995 article publications.

(D) Expenditures on R&D as a percentage of the GNP, data for the latest year available 1987-1997 [World Bank, World Development Indicators 2000, http://www.worldbank.org/data/wdi2000/pdfs/tab5_12.pdf] Additional data (indicated in italics) obtained from varied sources including the 1998 World Science Report and are for the most recent year accessible.

(E) The number of scientific research institutions (universities, institutes, etc.) per million population [Research Centers and Services Directories, The Gale Group, http://galenet.gale.com/a/acp/db/rcsd and World Bank, World Development Indicators 2000, http://www.worldbank.org/data/wdi2000/pdfs/tab2_1.pdf]

(F) Total number of US patents filed 1997-1999 and EPO Patents filed 1992-1994 by Citizens of the Country (most recent years available) ["Patent Counts by Country/State and Year, All Patents, All Types, Jan 1, 1977-Dec 21, 1999" USPTO, DOC, March 2000 and "Second European Report on Science and Technology Indicators" S-59, December 1997, EUR 17639]

(G) Total Number of US F-1 and J-1 Student Visas issued minus 3/4 the number of student visas converted to US permanent resident status in 1998 [US State Department Internet Site, Data for FY 1997, http://travel.state.gov/1997niv.pdf and US Immigration and Naturalization Service Statistical Yearbook 1998, http://www.ins.gov/graphics/aboutins/statistics/imm98.pdf] Canadian number from parliamentary debate on the subject (1998) since visa numbers do not correctly reflect student exchange between the two countries.

(H) Values from the corresponding column (A through G) converted to a comparative index by determining the number of standard deviations which the value of the national characteristic is away from the international average. Positive values indicate that the nation's value exceeds the international average.

(I) Weighted values of the scaled index parameters (seven columns labeled H) using the weighting factors at the top of the column to generate each factor's contribution to the overall scientific capacity index.

(J) Overall Index of Scientific Capacity - calculated as a sum of the weighted factor values (seven columns labeled I)

Values indicated in reduced boldface came from a number of unofficial Internet sources and should, at best, be considered educated estimates.

* indicates OECD member states

Figure A.1—continued

Appendix B. Questions Guiding Discussions and Interviews

Questions on Past or Current Collaboration

1. What was the subject of the project?

2. When did this project take place? For how long?

3. How many researchers did it involve on the U.S. side? The Korean side?

4. Did the project involve graduate students on the U.S. side? Korean side?

5. Do you know if the collaborator(s) in Korea had received academic/professional training in the United States?

6. Why did you choose to collaborate with this (these) foreign researchers/institutions?

   a. Presence of expertise/facilities/equipment in Korea?

   b. Korea provides unique conditions or access to unique resources (e.g., climate, ecology, human communities) for researcher?

   c. Common and complementary experiments and data exchange?

   d. Access to a unique data set?

   e. Research requires global/international partnerships?

   f. Others that you could state/briefly describe?

7. How did the two sides identify each other as potential collaborators?

8. Is this project a bilateral or multilateral effort?

9. How was this project funded? (NSF? Joint funding? Foundation grants?)

10. What were the methods you used to exchange information, and which were most crucial to the success of the project? (i.e., Internet, Web, fax)

11. Would this project have been possible without foreign collaboration?

Questions on Future Collaboration

1. Do you have plans to continue or initiate new collaborations with scientists and engineers in Korea?

2. Why? Why not?

3. What, in your opinion, are the fields/areas for stronger Korean-U.S. S&T cooperation in the next decade?

   a. Bilateral:

   b. Multinational:

4. What institutional and/or structural changes, in your opinion, would help to advance Korean-U.S. S&T cooperation in these fields/areas?

   - Other comments on collaboration:
   - Institutional issues:
   - Communication issues:
   - Cultural issues:
   - Issues unique to nature/features of the research collaboration:
   - Other issues:

Appendix C. Contact Information:
U.S. Government Agencies

Table C.1

Contact Information: U.S. Government Agencies

U.S. Federal Government Agency	R&D Budget: Total FY00 ($K)	Institute, Division, Directorate, or Program	Principal Officer (as of Spring 2002)	Contact Information	Website (as of Spring 2002)
Agency for International Development	$221,288	Bureau for Asia and the Near East Office of East and South Asian Affairs	Peter Lapera Director	Ronald Reagan Building 1300 Pennsylvania Ave., NW Washington, DC 20523 (202) 712-5529 pelapera@usaid.gov	http://www.usaid. gov/regions/ane
		Bureau for Asia and the Near East Office of East and South Asian Affairs	Cheryl Anderson Deputy Director, East Asia	Ronald Reagan Building 1300 Pennsylvania Ave., NW Washington, DC 20523 (202) 712-4107 chanderson@usaid.gov	http://www.usaid. gov/regions/ane
Department of Health and Human Services	$17,780,828	Office of the Secretary Office of Public Health and Science Office of Global Health Affairs	Thomas Novotny Director	5600 Fishers Lane Room 18-75 Rockville, MD 20857 (301) 443-1774 Fax: (301) 443-6288 tnovotny@osophs.dhhs.gov	www.globalhealth. gov/
		Office of the Deputy Secretary Office of the Chief of Staff Office of International Affairs	William Steiger Director	200 Independence Ave., SW Hubert Humphrey Building Washington, DC 20201 (202) 690-6174 Fax: (202) 712-4107 william.steiger@hhs.gov	http://www.hhs. gov/oia/intoffice. html

Table C.1—continued

U.S. Federal Government Agency	R&D Budget: Total FY00 ($K)	Institute, Division, Directorate, or Program	Principal Officer (as of Spring 2002)	Contact Information	Website (as of Spring 2002)
		Food & Drug Administration Office of International Programs	Walter Batts Acting Director	Parklawn Bldg. 5600 Fishers Lane Rockville, MD 20857 (301) 827-4553 Fax: (301) 827-1451	http://www.fda. gov/oia/ homepage.htm
		Food & Drug Administration Office of International Programs International Relations	Camille Brewer Acting Director	Parklawn Bldg. 5600 Fishers Lane Rockville, MD 20857 (301) 827-4480 Fax: (301) 827-0003 CBREWER@CFSAN.FDA.GOV	http://www.fda. gov/oia/ homepage.htm
		Food & Drug Administration Office of International Programs International Relations Asia and the Pacific	Julia Ho Associate Director	Parklawn Bldg. 5600 Fishers Lane Rockville, MD 20857 (301) 827-4480 Fax: (301) 827-0003 JHO@OC.FDA.GOV	http://www.fda. gov/oia/ homepage.htm
		Food & Drug Administration Office of International Programs International Planning and Resource Management	Beverly Corey Director	Parklawn Bldg. 5600 Fishers Lane Rockville, MD 20857 (301) 827-3430 Fax: (301) 480-1566 BCOREY@OC.FDA.GOV	http://www.fda. gov/oia/ homepage.htm

Table C.1—continued

U.S. Federal Government Agency	R&D Budget: Total FY00 ($K)	Institute, Division, Directorate, or Program	Principal Officer (as of Spring 2002)	Contact Information	Website (as of Spring 2002)
		Food & Drug Administration Office of International Programs International Planning and Resource Management Technical Cooperation/Technical Assistance	Barbara Ward-Groves Associate Director	Parklawn Bldg. 5600 Fishers Lane Rockville, MD 20857 (301) 827-0029 Fax: (301) 480-1566 BGROVES@OC.FDA.GOV	http://www.fda. gov/oia/ homepage.htm
		Food & Drug Administration Office of International Programs International Agreements	Lois Beaver Acting Director	Parklawn Bldg. 5600 Fishers Lane Rockville, MD 20857 (301) 827-3344 Fax: (301) 480-0716 LBEAVER1@OC.FDA.GOV	http://www.fda. gov/oia/ homepage.htm
		Food & Drug Administration Office of International Programs International Scientific Activities and Standards Staff	Vacant Director	Parklawn Bldg. 5600 Fishers Lane Rockville, MD 20857 (301) 827-6615 Fax: (301) 480-0814	http://www.fda. gov/oia/ homepage.htm

Table C.1—continued

U.S. Federal Government Agency	R&D Budget: Total FY00 ($K)	Institute, Division, Directorate, or Program	Principal Officer (as of Spring 2002)	Contact Information	Website (as of Spring 2002)
		National Institutes of Health National Cancer Institute Office of International Affairs	Federico Welsch Director	Executive Plaza North 6130 Executive Blvd. Suite 100 Bethesda, MD 20892 (301) 496-4761 Fax: (301) 496-3954 fw11x@nih.gov	http://www.nci. nih.gov/ AboutNci/OIA
		National Institutes of Health National Cancer Institute Office of International Affairs	James McKearney International Programs Officer	Executive Plaza North 6130 Executive Blvd. Suite 100 Bethesda, MD 20892 (301) 496-6344 jm141x@nih.gov	http://www.nci. nih.gov/ AboutNci/OIA
		National Institutes of Health National Eye Institute Office of International Program Activities	Vacant	(301) 496-4308	
		National Institutes of Health National Heart, Lung, and Blood Institute Office of Science and Technology	Carl Roth Director	9000 Rockville Pike Bethesda, MD 20892 (301) 496-6331 Fax: (301) 402-1056	http://www.nhlbi. nih.gov/index. htm
		National Institutes of Health National Heart, Lung, and Blood Institute Office of Science and Technology Office of International Programs	Ruth Hegyeli Director	9000 Rockville Pike Bethesda, MD 20892 (301) 496-5375 Fax: (301) 402-1056	http://www.nhlbi. nih.gov/index. htm

Table C.1—continued

U.S. Federal Government Agency	R&D Budget: Total FY00 ($K)	Institute, Division, Directorate, or Program	Principal Officer (as of Spring 2002)	Contact Information	Website (as of Spring 2002)
		National Institutes of Health Fogarty International Center Office of the Director Division of International Relations	Minerva Rojo Director	9000 Rockville Pike Bethesda, MD 20892 (301) 496-1415 Fax: (301) 402-2173	
		National Institutes of Health Fogarty International Center Office of the Director Division of International Relations East Asia and the Pacific	J. Allen Holt Program Officer	9000 Rockville Pike Bethesda, MD 20892 (301) 496-2516 Fax: (301) 402-2056	http://www.nih. gov/fic/regional/ pacific.html
Department of Housing and Urban Development	$50,000	Policy Development & Research Office of the Assistant Secretary for Policy Development and Research Office of International Affairs	Shannon Sorzano Deputy Assistant Secretary	451 Seventh St, SW Washington, DC 20410 (202) 708-0770 ext. 5931 Fax: (202) 708-5536	www.hud.gov/
Department of Interior	$583,683	U.S. Geological Survey Biological Resources Division Office of the Chief Scientist	Susan Haseltine Chief Scientist	12201 Sunrise Valley Drive Reston, VA 20192 (703) 648-4060 Fax: (703) 648-4039 susan_haseltine@usgs.gov	
		U.S. Geological Survey Geologic Division Scientific Programs	Jean Weaver International Programs Group Chief	12201 Sunrise Valley Drive Reston, VA 20192 (703) 648-6012 jweaver@usgs.gov	

Table C.1—continued

U.S. Federal Government Agency	R&D Budget: Total FY00 ($K)	Institute, Division, Directorate, or Program	Principal Officer (as of Spring 2002)	Contact Information	Website (as of Spring 2002)
National Science Foundation	$2,655,593	Directorate for Social, Behavioral and Economic Sciences International Programs Division East Asia and Pacific Program	Alexander DeAngelis Regional Coordinator	4201 Wilson Boulevard Arlington, VA 22230 (703) 292-8704 Fax: (703) 292-9175 adeangel@nsf.gov	http://www.nsf. gov/sbe/int/ eap/start.htm
		Directorate for Social, Behavioral and Economic Sciences International Programs Division East Asia and Pacific Program	Junku Yuh Program Manager (Korea)	4201 Wilson Boulevard Arlington, VA 22230 (703) 292-8704 Fax: (703) 292-9175 jyuh@nsf.gov	http://www.nsf. gov/sbe/int/ eap/start.htm
Department of State	N/A	Bureau of East Asian and Pacific Affairs	Anthony Hutchinson Country Officer	2201 C Street, NW Washington, DC 20520 (202) 647-7059	
		Bureau of East Asian and Pacific Affairs	John Mudge Economic Officer	2201 C Street, NW Washington, DC 20520 (202) 647-7718	
		Bureau of East Asian and Pacific Affairs	Joy O. Yamamoto Political Officer	2201 C Street, NW Washington, DC 20520 (202) 647-6706	

Table C.1—continued

U.S. Federal Government Agency	R&D Budget: Total FY00 ($K)	Institute, Division, Directorate, or Program	Principal Officer (as of Spring 2002)	Contact Information	Website (as of Spring 2002)
		Bureau of Oceans and International Environmental and Scientific Affairs Office of Science and Technology Cooperation	William R. Gaines Director		
Department of Agriculture	$1,552,000	Natural Resources and Environment Natural Resources Conservation Service Science and Technology	Lawrence Clark Deputy Chief	1400 Independence Ave., SW Washington, DC 20250 (202) 720-4630 Fax: (202) 720-7710 lawrence.clark@usda.gov	http://www.info.usda.gov/nrcs/SandT
		Natural Resources and Environment Forest Service International Programs	Valdis Mezainis Director	201 14th Street, SW Washington, DC 20090-6090 (202) 205-1650	http://www.fs.fed.us/global
		Natural Resources and Environment Forest Service International Programs	Alex Moad Assistant Director, Technical Cooperation	201 14th Street, SW Washington, DC 20090-6090 (202) 273-0163	http://www.fs.fed.us/global
		Farm and Foreign Agricultural Services International Cooperation & Development	Jocelyn Brown Assistant Deputy Administrator	South Agriculture Bldg. 1400 Independence Ave., SW Washington, DC 20250 (202) 690-0775 Fax: (202) 720-6103 brown@fas.usda.gov	

Table C.1—continued

U.S. Federal Government Agency	R&D Budget: Total FY00 ($K)	Institute, Division, Directorate, or Program	Principal Officer (as of Spring 2002)	Contact Information	Website (as of Spring 2002)
		Farm and Foreign Agricultural Services International Cooperation & Development Research & Scientific Exchanges Division	Carol Kramer-LeBlanc Director	South Agriculture Bldg. 1400 Independence Ave., SW Washington, DC 20250 (202) 720-4872 Fax: (202) 690-0892 kramer-leblanc@fas.usda.gov	
Department of Commerce	$950,168	Technology Administration Office of Technology Policy Office of International Technology	Cathleen Campbell Director	Herbert Clark Hoover Bldg. 14th St. & Constitution Ave., NW Washington, DC 20230 (202) 482-6351 Fax: (202) 501-6849 cathleen.campbell@ta.doc.gov	http://www.ta.doc. gov/International /Default.htm
		Technology Administration Office of Technology Policy Office of International Technology	Sharon Yun Policy Analyst (Korea)	Herbert Clark Hoover Bldg. 14th St. & Constitution Ave., NW Washington, DC 20230 (202) 482-6351 Fax: (202) 501-6849 sharon.yun@ta.doc.gov	http://www.ta.doc. gov/International /Default.htm
		Technology Administration Asia-Pacific Technology Program	Phyllis Yoshida Director	Herbert Clark Hoover Bldg. 14th St. & Constitution Ave., NW Washington, DC 20230 (202) 482-1287 phyllis.yoshida@ta.doc.gov	

Table C.1—continued

U.S. Federal Government Agency	R&D Budget: Total FY00 ($K)	Institute, Division, Directorate, or Program	Principal Officer (as of Spring 2002)	Contact Information	Website (as of Spring 2002)
		National Institute of Standards and Technology Office of International and Academic Affairs	Stephen Carpenter Director	100 Bureau Drive Stop 1090 Gaithersburg, MD 20899 (301) 975-4119 Fax: (301) 975-3530 b.carpenter@nist.gov	http://www.nist. gov/oiaa/oiaa1. htm
		National Institute of Standards and Technology Office of International and Academic Affairs	Claire Saudry Chief, International Affairs	100 Bureau Drive Gaithersburg, MD 20899 (301) 975-2386 claire.saundry@nist.gov	
		National Institute of Standards and Technology Office of International and Academic Affairs	Magdalena Navarro International Affairs Officer	100 Bureau Drive Gaithersburg, MD 20899 (301) 975-2130 magdalena.navarro@nist.gov	
		National Oceanic & Atmospheric Administration Oceanic & Atmospheric Research Office of Global Programs Climate Observations, Austral-Asia Region	Sydney Thurston	1100 Wayne Avenue Suite 1210 Silver Spring, MD 20910 (301) 427-2089 Fax: (301)-427-2073 sidney.thurston@noaa.gov	http://www.ogp. noaa.gov/ aboutogp/index. html
Department of Education	$233,000	International Affairs Division	Lenore Garcia	Room 6W108 400 Maryland Avenue, SW Washington, DC 20202-8401 (202) 401-0430 Fax: (202) 401-2508 lenore.garcia@ed.gov	

Table C.1—continued

U.S. Federal Government Agency	R&D Budget: Total FY00 ($K)	Institute, Division, Directorate, or Program	Principal Officer (as of Spring 2002)	Contact Information	Website (as of Spring 2002)
		Office of Post-Secondary Education Higher Education Programs International Education and Graduate Program Services	Ralph Hines Director	1900 K St., NW Washington, DC 20006 (202) 502-7700 Fax: (202) 502-7852 ralph.hines@ed.gov	http://www.ed. gov/offices/ OPE/HEP/
Department of Energy	$6,196,684	Office of Nuclear Energy, Science and Technology Office of Technology and International Cooperation	Shane Johnson Associate Director	19901 Germantown Road Germantown, MD 20874-1290 (301) 903-3860 (301) 903-5057 shane.johnson@hq.doe.gov	
		Office of Policy and International Affairs Office of Policy Office of Science and Technology Policy Analysis	Robert Marlay Director	Forrestal Building 1000 Independence Ave., SW Washington, DC 20585 (202) 586-3949 Fax: (202) 586-5342 robert.marlay@hq.doe.gov	http://www. pi.energy.gov/
		Office of Policy and International Affairs Office of International Energy Policy	David Pumphrey Deputy Assistant Secretary	Forrestal Building 1000 Independence Ave., SW Washington, DC 20585 (202) 586-5800 Fax: (202) 586-0861 david.pumphrey@hq.doe.gov	http://www. pi.energy.gov/

Table C.1—continued

U.S. Federal Government Agency	R&D Budget: Total FY00 ($K)	Institute, Division, Directorate, or Program	Principal Officer (as of Spring 2002)	Contact Information	Website (as of Spring 2002)
		Office of Policy and International Affairs Office of International Energy Cooperation Office of European and Asian Affairs	Robert Price Director	1000 Independence Ave., SW Washington, DC 20585 (202) 586-6130 Fax: (202) 586-1180 robert.s.price@hq.doe.gov	http://www. pi.energy.gov // asia.html
		Office of Policy and International Affairs Office of International Energy Cooperation Office of International Science and Technology Cooperation	Barry Gale Director	Forrestal Building 1000 Independence Ave., SW Washington, DC 20585 (202) 586-6708 Fax: (202) 586-1180 barry.gale@hq.doe.gov	http://www. pi.energy.gov /
		Office of Policy and International Affairs Office of International Energy Cooperation Office of International Science and Technology Cooperation	Keena Hillary Program Analyst	Forrestal Building 1000 Independence Ave., SW Washington, DC 20585 (202) 586-8156 Fax: (202) 586-1180 keena.hillary@hq.doe.gov	http://www. pi.energy.gov /
		Under Secretary for Energy, Science, and Environment Office of Science	Raymond Orbach Director	Forrestal Building 1000 Independence Ave., SW Washington, DC 20585 (202) 586-5430 (202) 586-4120 ray.orbach@science.doe.gov	http://www.sc.doe. gov /

Table C.1—continued

U.S. Federal Government Agency	R&D Budget: Total FY00 ($K)	Institute, Division, Directorate, or Program	Principal Officer (as of Spring 2002)	Contact Information	Website (as of Spring 2002)
Environmental Protection Agency	$536,800	Office of International Activities	Judith Elizabeth Ayres Assistant Administrator	Ariel Rios Federal Building 1200 Pennsylvania Ave., NW Washington, DC 20004 (202) 564-6600 ayres.judithe@epa.gov	http://www.epa. gov/oia/
		Office of International Activities Office of Technology Cooperation & Assistance	Sylvia Correa Director	Ariel Rios Federal Building 1200 Pennsylvania Ave., NW Washington, DC 20004 (202) 564-6443 correa.sylvia@epa.gov	http://www.epa. gov/oia/

Bibliography

Amsden, Alice, *Asia's Next Giant: South Korea and Late Industrialization*, New York, Oxford University Press, 1989.

Amsden, Alice, *The Rise of the Rest: Challenges to the West from Late Industrializing Economies*, New York: Oxford University Press, 2001.

Amsden, Alice, Ted Tschang, and Akira Goto, "Do Foreign Companies Conduct R&D in Developing Countries?" ADB Institute Working Paper, No. 14, March 2001.

Andersson, Thomas, and Carl Dahlman, *Korea and the Knowledge-based Economy: Making the Transition*, Paris: Organization for Economic Cooperation and Development, 2001.

Archibugi, D., J. Howells, and J. Michie, eds., *Innovation Policy in a Global Economy*, Cambridge, England: Cambridge University Press, 1999.

Beaver, Donald de B. "Reflections on Scientific Collaboration (and Its Study): Past, Present and Prospective," Keynote lecture delivered at the Second Berlin Workshop on Scientometrics and Informetrics/Collaboration in Science and in Technology, held in Berlin, September 1–4, 2000.

Beaver, Donald de B., and R. Rosen, "Studies in Scientific Collaboration." Part I. "The Professional Origins of Scientific Co-authorship," in *Scientometrics*, No. 1, 1978, pp. 65–84; Part II. "Scientific Co-authorship, Research Productivity, and Visibility in the French Elite," *Scientometrics*, No. 1, 1979, pp. 133–149.

Ben-David, Joseph, *The Scientist's Role in Society: A Comparative Study*, Englewood Cliffs, New Jersey: Prentice-Hall, 1971.

Blume, Stuart, *The Social Direction of the Public Science: Causes and Consequences of Co-operation Between Scientists and Non-Scientific Groups*, Dordrecht, Holland: Reidel, 1987.

Boehme, Gernot, and Nico Stehr, eds., *The Knowledge Society: The Growing Impact of Scientific Knowledge on Social Relations*, Dordrecht, Holland: Reidel, 1986.

Carnegie Commission on Science, Technology, and Government, *Partnerships for Global Development: The Clearing Horizon*, New York: Carnegie Corporation, December 1992.

Choi, Youngrak, Hwe-Ik Zhang, and Sungsoo Song, *Monitoring S&T Activities in Korea as a Follow-up of the "World Conference on Science,"* STEPI, 2001. [Korean]

Choung, Jae-Yong, and Hye-Ran Hwang, "National Systems of Innovation: Institutional Linkages and Performances in the Case of Korea and Taiwan," *Scientometrics*, Vol. 48, No. 3, 2000, pp. 413–442.

Chung, SungChul, *Trends and Task of Science and Technology International Cooperation Policy*, STEPI, 2000. [Korean]

Chung, SungChul, *A Study on Basic Policy Framework for International Scientific and Technological Cooperation*, STEPI, 2001. [Korean]

Chung, SungChul, "International S&T Cooperation: Korea Study (Preliminary Results)," a presentation to the Global Science Forum, Paris, January 2002.

Crawford, Elisabeth T., *Nationalism and Internationalism in Science, 1880–1939: Four Studies of the Nobel Population*, New York: Cambridge University Press, 1992.

Crawford, Elisabeth T., and Stein Rokkan, eds., *Sociological Praxis: Current Roles and Settings*, London: Sage Publications, 1976.

Crawford, Elisabeth T., Terry Shinn, and Sverker Sörlin, eds., *Denationalizing Science: The Contexts of International Scientific Practice*, Dordrecht, Holland: Kluwer Academic Publishers, 1993.

Dalton, D. H., M. G. Serapio, and P. G. Yoshida, *Globalizing Industrial Research and Development*, U.S. Department of Commerce, Office of Technology Policy, 1999.

Doré, Jean-Christopher, Tiiu Ojasoo, and Yoshiko Okubo, "Correspondence Factorial Analysis of the Publication Patterns of 48 Countries over the Period 1981–1992," *Journal of the American Society for Information Science*, Vol. 47, No. 8, 1996, pp. 588–602.

Elias, Norbert, Herminio Martins, and Richard Whitley, eds., *Scientific Establishments and Hierarchies*, Dordrecht, Holland: Reidel, 1982.

Florida, Richard, "Other Countries' Money," *Technology Review*, March–April, 1998.

Frame, J. Davidson, and Mark P. Carpenter, "International Research Collaboration," *Social Studies of Science*, Vol. 9, 1979, pp. 481–497.

Fuller, Steve, et al., *The Cognitive Turn: Sociological and Psychological Perspective on Science*, Dordrecht, Holland: Kluwer Academic Publishers, 1989.

Gaillard, Jacques, "North-South Partnerships: Is Collaboration Possible Between Unequal Partners?" *Knowledge and Policy*, Vol. 7, No. 2, Summer 1994, pp. 31–63.

Genest, Christian, and Carl Thibault, "Investigating the Concentration Within a Research Community Using Joint Publications and Coauthorship via Intermediaries," *Scientometrics*, Vol. 51, No. 2, 2001, pp. 429–440.

Georghiou, Luke, "Global Cooperation in Research," *Research Policy*, Vol. 27, 1998, pp. 611–626.

Gibbons, M., et al., *The New Production of Knowledge: The Dynamics of Science and Research in Contemporary Societies*, London, England: Sage Publications, 1994.

Glänzel, Wolfgang, "Double Effort = Double Impact? A Critical View at International Coauthorship in Chemistry," *Scientometrics*, Vol. 50 No. 2, 2001a, pp. 199–214. [abstract]

Glänzel, Wolfgang, "National Characteristics in International Scientific Coauthorship Relations," *Scientometrics*, Vol. 51, No. 1, 2001b, pp. 69–115.

Graham, Loren, and Wolf Lepenies, eds., *Functions and Uses of Disciplinary Histories*, Dordrecht, Holland: Reidel, 1983.

Gusmao, Regina, "Developing and Using Indicators of Multinational S&T Cooperation for Policymaking: The Experience from European Research Programmes," *Scientometrics*, Vol. 47, No. 3, 2000, pp. 493–514.

Institute for Development Studies, *Selected Review of International Institutes Supporting Development Research, European Foundation for Research on Development, Issues and Opinions Study*, Brighton, United Kingdom: University of Sussex, 2000.

International Institute for Management Development (IMD), World Competitiveness Yearbook, 2000, www02.imd.ch/wcy.

Jankowski, John, "R&D: Foundations for Innovation," *Research Technology Management*, Vol. 41, No. 2, March–April 1998.

Kang, Nam-Hoon, and Kentaro Sakai, *International Alliances: Their Role in Industrial Globalization*, OECD, STI Working Paper, 2000.

Kauffman, Stuart, *At Home in the Universe: The Search for Laws of Self-Organization and Complexity*, New York: Oxford University Press, 1995.

Kim, Ki-Kook, Sung-Bum Hong, and Byung-Sun Kim, *An Exploratory Study on the Multinational's R&D Activities in Korea*, STEPI, 1999. [Korean]

Kim, Ki-Kook, Deok-Soon Yim, Myung-Jin Lee, and Sung-Bum Hong, *Survey for R&D Activities of Foreign Firms in Korea*, STEPI, 2000. [Korean]

Kim, M. J., "Korean International Coauthorship in Science 1994–1996," *Journal of Information Science*, No. 25, 1999, pp. 403–412.

Kim, Mee-Jean, "A Bibliometric Analysis of Physics Publications in Korea, 1994–1998," *Scientometrics*, Vol. 50, No. 3, 2000, pp. 503–521.

Knorr-Cetina, Karen, *The Manufacture of Knowledge: An Essay on the Constructivist and Contextual Nature of Science*, Oxford: Pergamon Press, 1981.

Krohn, Wolfgang, Guenter Kueppers, and Helga Nowotny, *Self-Organisation: Portrait of a Scientific Revolution*, Dordrecht, Holland: Kluwer Academic Publishers, 1990.

Leclerc, Michel, Yoshiko Okubo, Luiz Frigoletto, and Jean-Francois Miquel, "Scientific Co-operation Between Canada and the European Community," *Science and Public Policy*, Vol. 19, No. 1, February 1992, pp. 15–24.

Lee, Myung-Jin, *Study on Utilization of International Mega-Science Projects*, STEPI, 2001. [Korean]

Leydesdorff, Loet, "Problems with the 'Measurement' of National Scientific Performance," *Science and Public Policy*, No. 15, 1998, pp. 149–152.

Leydesdorff, Loet, "Is the European Union Becoming a Single Publication System?" *Scientometrics*, Vol. 47, No. 2, 2000.

Leydesdorff, Loet, The Challenge of Scientometrics: The Development, Measurement, and Self-Organisation of Scientific Communications, Universal Publishers/uPublish.com, USA, 2001.

Leydesdorff, Loet, "A Sociological Theory of Communication: The Self-Organisation of the Knowledge-Based Society," Universal Publishers/uPublish.com, USA, 2001.

Luukkonen, Terttu, Olle Persson, and Gunnar Sivertsen, "Understanding Patterns of International Scientific Collaboration," *Science, Technology, & Human Values*, Vol. 17, No. 1, Winter 1992, pp. 101–126.

MacLeod, R., ed., *The Commonwealth of Science*, Melbourne, Australia: Oxford University Press, 1988.

Mély, B., M. Abd El Kader, G. Dudognon, and Y. Okubo, "Scientific Publications of China in 1994: Evolution or Revolution?" *Scientometrics*, Vol. 42, No. 1, 1998, pp. 3–16.

Mendelsohn, Everett, Peter Weingart, and Richard Whitley, eds., *The Social Production of Scientific Knowledge*, Dordrecht, Holland: Reidel, 1977.

Meyer-Krahmer, F., "Internationalisation of Research and Technology: Trends, Issues, and Implications for Science and Technology Policies in Europe," Brussels, Belgium: European Commission ETAN Papers Collection, 1998.

Mitchell, Graham, *Korea's Strategy for Leadership in Research and Development*, U.S. Department of Commerce, Office of Technology Policy, June 1997.

MOST, Results of Examination, Analysis and Evaluation of the Year 1999 National R&D Projects, MOST, 2000a. [Korean]

MOST, Vision 2025: Korea's Long-Term Plan for Science and Technology Development, MOST, 2000b. [English]

MOST, Implementation Plan for Science and Technology Internationalization Projects, MOST, 2002. [Korean]

MOST, Main Science & Technology Indicators, http://www.most.go.kr/research-e/body.html. [English]

MOST, Science & Technology Policy, http://www.most.go.kr/policy-e/body.html. [English]

Miquel, J. F., T. Ojasoo, Y. Okubo, A. Paul, and J. C. Doré, "World Science in 18 Disciplinary Areas: Comparative Evaluation of the Publication Patterns of 48

Countries over the Period 1981–1992," *Scientometrics*, Vol. 33, 1995, pp. 149–167.

Miquel, J. F., and Y. Okubo, "Structure of International Collaboration in Science—Part II: Comparisons of Profiles in Countries Using a Link Indicator," *Scientometrics*, Vol. 29, No. 2, 1994, pp. 271–297.

Mowery, David C., and Nathan Rosenberg, *Technology and the Pursuit of Economic Growth*, Cambridge, England: Cambridge University Press, 1989.

National Research Council, *Scientific and Technological Cooperation Among Industrialized Countries: The Role of the U.S.*, Washington, D.C.: National Academy Press, 1984.

National Science Board, *Science and Engineering Indicators—2000*, National Science Foundation, 2000.

National Science Board, *Science and Engineering Indicators—2002*, National Science Foundation, 2002.

National Science and Technology Council (Korea), *Implementation Strategies for Science and Technology Internationalization*, National Science and Technology Council, 2001.

National Science and Technology Council (Korea), Homepage, http://www.nstc.go.kr

Narin, Francis, "Globalisation of Research, Scholarly Information, and Patents—Ten Year Trends," Proceedings of the North American Serials Interest Group (NASIF) 6th Annual Conference, June 14–17, 1991, *The Serials Librarian*, Vol. 21, Nos. 2–3, 1991.

Nowotny, Helga, and Hilary Rose, eds., *Counter-Movements in the Sciences: The Sociology of the Alternatives to Big Science*, Dordrecht, Holland: Reidel, 1979.

Okubo, Y., J. C. Doré, T. Ojasoo, and J. F. Miquel, "A Multivariate Analysis of Publication Trends in the 1980s with Special Reference to South-East Asia," *Scientometrics*, Vol. 41, No. 3, 1998, pp. 273–289.

Okubo, Yoshiko, *Bibliometric Indicators and Analysis of Research Systems: Methods and Examples*, Paris, France: Organisation for Economic Co-operation and Development (OECD), 1997.

Okubo, Y., J. F. Miquel, L. Frigoletto, and J. C. Doré, "Structure of International Collaboration in Science: Typology of Countries Through Multivariate Techniques Using a Link Indicator," *Scientometrics*, Vol. 25, No. 2, 1992, pp. 321–351.

Organisation for Economic Co-operation and Development (OECD), *Reviews of National Science and Technology Policy: Republic of Korea*, Paris, France: OECD, 1996.

Organisation for Economic Co-operation and Development (OECD), *The Global Research Village: How Information and Communication Technologies Affect the Science System,* Paris, France: OECD, 1998.

Organisation for Economic Co-operation and Development (OECD), *Science, Technology and Industry Scoreboard 2001,* Paris, France: OECD, 2001.

Price, D. de S., *Little Science, Big Science—and Beyond,* New York: Columbia University Press, 1986.

Science and Technology Agency—Japanese Government, *White Paper on Science and Technology, Striving to Become a Front-Runner in Research Activity, 1996,* Tokyo, Japan: Japan Science and Technology Corporation, 1996.

Salomon, Jean-Jacques, "The 'Internationale' of Science," *Science Studies* I, 1971, pp. 23–42.

Salomon, Jean-Jacques, "Scientists and International Relations: A European Perspective," *Technology in Society,* Vol. 23, 2001, pp. 291–315.

Salomon, Jean-Jacques, Francisco R. Sagasti, and Céline Sachs-Jeantet, eds., *The Uncertain Quest: Science, Technology, and Development,* Tokyo, Japan: United Nations University Press, 1994.

Schubert, A., and T. Braun, "International Collaboration in the Sciences, 1981—1985," *Scientometrics,* Vol. 19, 1990, pp. 3–10.

Schubert, A., W. Glänzel, and T. Braun, "Scientometric Datafiles. A Comprehensive Set of Indicators on 2649 Journals and 96 Countries in All Major Science Fields and Subfields 1981–1985," *Scientometrics,* Vol. 16, Nos. 1–6, 1989, pp. 3–478.

Skolnikoff, Eugene, *The Elusive Transformation,* Princeton, NJ: Princeton University Press, 1993.

Skolnikoff, Eugene, "The Political Role of Scientific Cooperation," *Technology in Society,* Vol. 23, 2001, pp. 461–471.

Smith, Bruce L. R., and Claude Barfield, eds., *Technology, R&D, and the Economy,* Washington, DC: The Brookings Institution and the American Enterprise Institute, 1996.

Smith, David, and J. Sylvan Katz, *Collaborative Approaches to Research, HEFCE Fund Review of Research Policy and Funding,* Final Report, Brighton, United Kingdom: University of Sussex, April 2000.

Stein, Josephine, *External Relations in the European Union, the United States and Japan and International Research and Technological Development Cooperation,* Manchester, United Kingdom: Policy Research in Engineering Science and Technology (PREST), July 1999.

Thorsteinsdottie, O. Halla, "External Research Collaboration in Two Small Science Systems," *Scientometrics,* Vol. 49, No. 1, 2000, pp. 145–160. [abstract]

Van den Besselaar, Peter, "The Cognitive and the Social Structure of STS," Scientometrics, Vol. 51, No. 2., pp. 441–460. [abstract]

Van Raan, Anthony F. J., "Science as an International Enterprise," *Science and Public Policy*, No. 24, 1997, pp. 290–300.

Van Raan, Anthony F. J., "Evaluating the Scientific Excellence of Research Programmes: a Pivot of Decision-Making," *The IPTS Report*, No. 40, December 1999, pp. 30–37.

Wagner, Caroline S., *International Cooperation in Research and Development: An Inventory of U.S. Government Spending and a Framework for Measuring Benefits*, Santa Monica, CA: RAND, MR-900-OSTP, 1997.

Wagner, Caroline S., *International Alliances and Technology Transfer: Challenging National Foresight?* Santa Monica, CA: RAND, RP-908, 1999.

Wagner, Caroline S., and Nurith Berstein, *U.S. Government Funding of Cooperative Research and Development in North America*, Santa Monica, CA: RAND, MR-1115-OSTP, 1999.

Wagner, Caroline, Irene Brahmakulam, Brian Jackson, Anny Wong, and Tatsuro Yoda, *Science and Technology Collaboration: Building Capacity in Developing Countries?* Santa Monica, CA: RAND, MR-1357.0-WB, 2001.

Wagner, Caroline S., Linda Staheli, Richard Silberglitt, Anny Wong, and James Kadtke, "Linking Effectively: Learning Lessons from Successful International Collaboration," Santa Monica, CA: RAND, DB-345, 2002.

Wagner, Caroline S., Allison Yezril, and Scott Hassell, *International Cooperation in Research and Development: An Update to an Inventory of U.S. Government Spending*, Santa Monica, CA: RAND, MR-1248, 2000.

Weiss, Charles, "Scientific and Technological Constraints to Economic Growth and Equity," in R. E. Evenson and G. Ranis, *Science and Technology: Lessons for Development Policy*, Boulder, CO: Westview Press, 1990.

Wong, P.-K., *Globalization of US-Japan Production Networks and the Growth of Singapore's Electronics Industry*, National University of Singapore, 1998.

Wong, P.-K., *National Innovation System for Rapid Technology Catch-Up: An Analytical Framework and a Comparative Analysis of Korea*, Taiwan and Singapore, Center for Management of Innovation and Technopreneurship, National University of Singapore, 1999.

World Bank Institute, *Korea and the Knowledge-Based Economy: Making the Transition*, Washington, DC: World Bank, February 2001.

Yn, Seonjae, and Dekd-Soon Yim, *A Policy Research on Korea's International Cooperative R&D Activities*, STEPI, 1999. [Korean]

Ziman, John, *Prometheus Bound: Science in a Dynamic Steady State*, Cambridge, England: Cambridge University Press, 1994.

Zitt, Michael, Elise Bassecoulard, and Yoshiko Okubo, "Shadows of the Past in International Cooperation: Collaboration Profiles of the Top Five Producers of Science," *Scientometrics*, Vol. 47, No. 3, 2000, pp. 627–657.